BLACK ROCK
AND
BLUE WATER

BLACK ROCK
AND
BLUE WATER

The Wreck of Royal Mail Ship
Rhone *in St. Narciso's*
Hurricane of October 1867

Andrew C. A. Jampoler

Naval Institute Press
Annapolis, Maryland

Naval Institute Press
291 Wood Road
Annapolis, MD 21402

First Naval Institute Press paperback edition published in 2017.

The Library of Congress has cataloged the eBook edition as follows:
Jampoler, Andrew C. A., date
   Black Rock and blue water: the great hurricane of October 1867 and the wreck of the Royal Mail Ship Rhone / Andrew C.A. Jampoler.
      1 online resource.
   Includes bibliographical references and index.
   Description based on print version record and CIP data provided by publisher; resource not viewed.
   ISBN 978-0-87021-040-2 (epub) -- ISBN 978-0-87021-040-2 (mobi) 1. Rhone (Ship) 2. Shipwrecks--British Virgin Islands. I. Title.
   G530.R359
   910.9163'65--dc23
                                    2013029694

25 24 23 22 21 20 19 18 17   9 8 7 6 5 4 3 2 1
First printing

CONTENTS

ILLUSTRATIONS

ACKNOWLEDGMENTS

In 2006 the six of us, my wife, Suzy, and I; our daughter and son-in-law, Chrissy and Bart; and our two granddaughters, Molly and Carly, dove on the wreck of the *Rhone*. Riding out to her underwater park in the British Virgin Islands under brilliant Caribbean skies, our boat captain told us the story of her shipwreck off Salt Island. What he didn't know, he glibly made up. True or false, all of it was fascinating, and that fascination triggered this short book.

Over the years that Terry Lilley, of Bromley, England, helped me to research this story, he has become a good friend as well as a great resource. I appreciate his friendship even more than I am grateful for his generous assistance. The late Stuart Nichol, an employee of Royal Mail Lines, Ltd., through the 1960s and the author of its two-volume history, *Macqueen's Legacy*, spent the last years of his life in Australia as the Royal Mail Steam Packet Company's volunteer historian and archivist. I owe him appreciation for his scholarship, especially as encapsulated in his extensive digital "RMSPC/RMLL Scrapbook," which sadly I will never be able to express. Julian Heming, tropical prediction scientist in the United Kingdom's Met Office, helpfully read and corrected errors in his specialty. Any that remain are my fault, not his.

1

The Millwall Ironworks and Shipbuilding Company

In the mid-nineteenth century, the swampy and foul-smelling Isle of Dogs beyond London's East End was not a natural island at all. It was a low-lying peninsula bound by the arc of a tight meander of the River Thames (the last great bend in the river as it left the capital for the North Sea, forty-one nautical miles downriver from London Bridge) and made into an island by cuts across its narrow neck. On what had been mostly windswept and boggy pastureland fifty years earlier, there now stood more than two dozen shipyards, dry docks, and steam-engine manufacturing factories, all served by "slushy, ill formed roads" and located amid stunted trees and "tumble-down buildings, stagnant ditches, and tracts of marshy, rubbish-filled waste ground." The great industrial complex that spread along the shoreline of this unlikely place, protected from regular tidal flooding by raised embankments, would be for a short while longer the heart of modern English iron shipbuilding and marine engineering.

Some 15,000 men and boys each labored almost seventy hours a week in works on the island. Thousands more were employed in other factories nearby. Scottish mechanics who first learned their trade in the yards packed along the Clyde River were the elite of these shipbuilding day laborers, drawn here from the north by better pay. Most of the rest were denizens of London's underclass, from Lancashire and Staffordshire. The island's masterwork was the huge—and hugely unsuccessful—passenger liner SS *Great Eastern* (1858); at 690 feet and

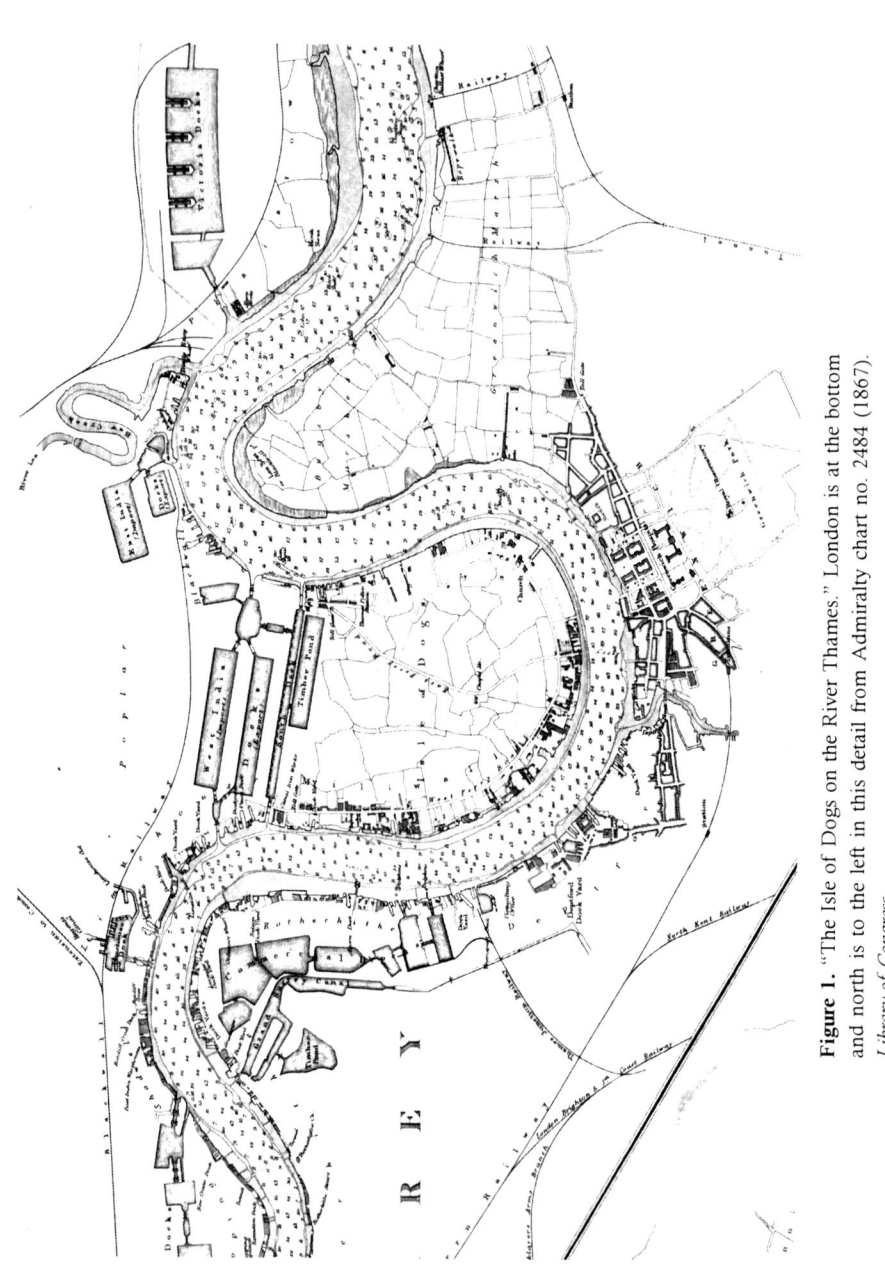

Figure 1. "The Isle of Dogs on the River Thames." London is at the bottom and north is to the left in this detail from Admiralty chart no. 2484 (1867). *Library of Congress.*

22,500 tons, she was the biggest merchant ship ever launched into the Thames River.

For a brief time in the mid-1860s, the Millwall Ironworks and Shipbuilding Company—its name recalled the windmills that once drove pumps to drain the site—was the largest of the shipyards on the island. Its works filled a twenty-seven-acre tract on its western side, spread along more than one-quarter mile of island frontage on the syrupy Thames. Located far from iron ore and coal deposits, the yard melted scrap metal in a great smelter, and its iron ships were assembled from frames and plates thriftily recycled from this stuff. On Millwall's large property and under thick clouds of steam, nearly five thousand men worked in the company's shops, rolling mills, forges, and slipways, building handsome oceangoing ships from the smoke and noise that seemed to be their chief materials.

A number of merchant vessels and a single Royal Navy ship, the *Monitor*-class ram HMS *Northumberland* (1866), came off the Millwall ways. *Northumberland*'s long-delayed launch (the 400-foot-long, heavily armored ship hung up on the slipway; it took expensive and embarrassing weeks to break her free) contributed to bankrupting the shipyard, but it might have been the bad luck of its manager, C. J. Mare, that really put Millwall under. He was given charge of Millwall after John Scott Russell retired in 1861, despite the fact that all three of Mare's earlier shipbuilding ventures appear to have come unraveled. In 1866 this one did, too, when the yard's financial backers collapsed.

Millwall was not alone in its distress, however; shipbuilding on the Thames, always a boom and bust business, fell on hard times after the mid-1860s. Economic cycles aside, the Isle of Dog's great distance from sources of essential raw materials eventually became a handicap that even ingenuity and hard labor could not overcome. The island's yards had dominated English shipbuilding for three decades, but once iron ships replaced wooden ones, shipyards on the Thames quickly lost contracts to competitors on Scotland's Clyde River and on the northeast coast that had the good fortune to be located closer to iron ore and coal mines.

Millwall was the home yard of the pretty 1,700-ton screw steamer, Royal Mail Ship *Rhone* (1865), built alongside the ill-starred *Northumberland* and the slightly smaller paddle steamer RMS *Danube* (also 1866, but delivered very late). Both steamers were owned and operated by the Royal Mail Steam Packet Company (RMSP). As it turned out, *Rhone* was delivered to the Royal Mail in the Indian summer of iron shipbuilding on the Thames, the short-lived boom of 1865–67. Just a few years later everything became very bleak. Yards closed and unemployment on the Isle of Dogs skyrocketed. A lethal midsummer cholera epidemic killed 12,000 in the East End. High food prices, possibly a consequence of a wetter than usual autumn, threatened the survivors with hunger. By 1868 nearly half of all working-class housing on the once-teeming island was vacant and abandoned; a pall settled over the place.

2

The Royal Mail Steam Packet Company

S oon after its accidental discovery by Columbus at the
end of the fifteenth century, and thanks to its real and
imagined riches, the Caribbean quickly became an arena
of intense European competition. The contest continued almost
into modern times, slowed only by an often lethal tropical
fever ("yellow fever," describing one symptom, "vomito
negro," describing another) that ruthlessly pruned the ranks of
vulnerable Europeans and of the remaining natives, who had
until then beaten the odds and managed to survive the usually
fatal impact of discovery by fervent Christians.

Despite horrific death rates from mysterious "noxious
Vapours and Distemperatures of the Air," the Caribbean was
important to England as a source of exotic tropical products—
sugar and rum, especially, but also spices, coffee, chocolate,
tobacco, and dyestuffs—and as a market for finished goods
from the metropolis. When the seventeenth century ended,
the West Indies were already so important and so promising
that monthly packet boat service between England and the
Caribbean was begun just a few years later, in 1704. (This first
scheduled service and its successors in 1745 and 1755 would
quickly fail, victims of rapacious pirates and enterprising
privateers as much as of business plan errors. A fourth attempt
in 1763 was finally successful in putting transatlantic service on
a permanent basis.)

By the early 1700s British imperial interests in the West
Indies were reflected in a string of well-developed Royal

Navy dockyards and hospitals in the Lesser Antilles supported by an elaborate transoceanic logistics system that delivered and stocked all the foodstuffs and stores essential to support a powerful navy squadron. In turn, the squadron guaranteed that Great Britain's political and commercial goals received due consideration in the furious scramble for advantage in the Western Hemisphere that characterized the 1700s and early 1800s. The British, at the beginning of the nineteenth century arguably the Old World's best (and, the Dutch now aside, its most aggressive) sailors, had already gained the advantage in this maritime theater over the Caribbean's first colonizers.

The same businesslike approach that kept the Royal Navy successfully deployed in distant waters worked to enrich England's industrialists and merchants. From a fairly narrow focus on their own possessions, Britain's commercial impetus and strategic objectives, as always dovetailed neatly together, eventually grew to encompass much of central and coastal South America. The best access to this expanding universe was by sea through the Caribbean, a route first opened at the end of the fifteenth century by those who followed Columbus, in sailing vessels riding the prevailing easterlies across the Atlantic, heading, their crews hoped, toward the beckoning riches of the Orient.

James Macqueen (1778–1870), from Lanarkshire, Scotland, had long experience in the West Indies, including twenty-three years spent as a young man managing a sugar plantation on Grenada and traveling throughout the islands. From this personal history must have come the germ of his idea. Macqueen's bold "General Plan," a proposal to replace the Royal Navy's sail-powered mail packet service to the Americas with steam vessels, was implemented generally as he conceived it, including a handsome annual subsidy from the government to make the expensive enterprise work and to keep investors in the business happy.

As planned by Macqueen, Royal Mail paddle steamers from Southampton would arrive at the RMSP's hub in the Western Hemisphere, where a fleet of small company vessels was already lying in wait. In a two-week marine version of the frantic two-hour passenger and baggage exchange of today's hub-and-spoke airline operations, people, mail, and cargo would be transferred across the decks of ships lashed together. Steamers would have their coal bunkers filled, and fresh water and food ("provender") would be loaded on board for the return trip. Once refueling, reprovisioning, and cleaning up after the messy exchange were completed, all ships would scatter back

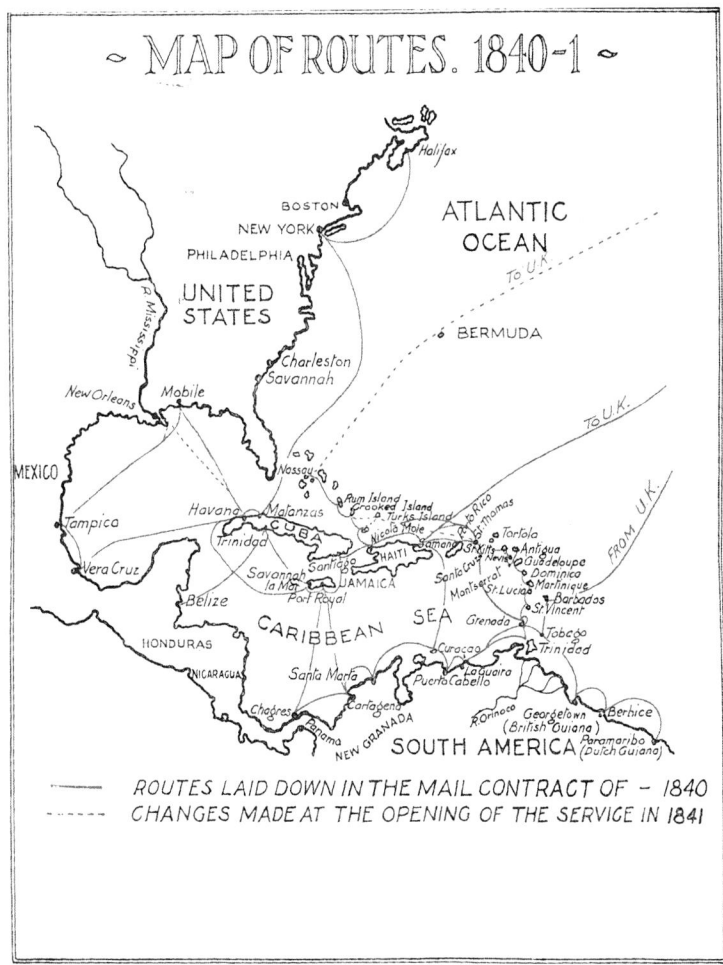

Figure 2. Map of Routes 1840–1. *From Bushnell,* Royal Mail, *10.*

up the same routes they had just come down. The complicated minuet would be repeated every two weeks, sustaining Great Britain's connection to the colonies and countries of the New World.

The company that grew from this plan quickly took its place alongside the Cunard Line (founded 1839) and the Peninsular and Oriental Steamship Company (founded in 1840 out of the Peninsular Steam Navigation Company) as one of the great arteries of British Empire. These names, "Cunard," "the P&O," and "the Royal Mail," together with several others, would become words to conjure with in an age of proud imperialism, one infatuated with the possibilities of scheduled travel to exotic places, and with the necessity of military deployment abroad.

Although Macqueen's plan actually predated the events by some months, it's probably not a coincidence that much of this ferment happened in the shadow of the first two westbound all-steam crossings of the Atlantic in April 1838. Until then "steamers" inevitably had resorted to sail to complete their crossings. *Sirius*'s and *Great Western*'s near-simultaneous demonstrations that steam could go all the way must have been a powerful fillip to technology enthusiasts of the day. (*Sirius*'s two crossings could be counted as a fluke. She was built to ply the Irish Sea and limped back to the British Isles after recoaling in New York only by burning her furniture. The paddle steamer *Great Western*—she carried 600 tons of coal and burned 452 on the first westbound crossing—continued back and forth across the Atlantic for nearly a decade. Later, in 1847, *Great Western* was bought into the Royal Mail fleet to replace the shipwrecked RMS *Tweed* on the Southampton–West Indies service and retired from it in 1856 to be broken up into firewood in Castle's yard at Vauxhall, England.)

Macqueen's original plan had company outstations as far east as Paramaribo, Dutch Guinea; as far south as Chagres (Colón), Panama; as far west as Tampico, Mexico; and as far north as Halifax, Nova Scotia. Service to the United States was included, too, through the ports of New York and Mobile. (New Orleans and Bermuda would soon be added and Mobile dropped.) The port of Charlotte Amalie, St. Thomas's island capital and the Caribbean gateway closest to Europe, was important from the outset; it grew to become the company's Caribbean hub after 1851.[1]

Charlotte Amalie, seen from the sea as clusters of brightly painted houses under red-tiled roofs climbing up hillsides, was lovely in the mid-nineteenth century. To European eyes it might have appeared to be Eden after the fall and following the onset of commercial development. English novelist Anthony Trollope, traveling on the Royal Mail Steam Packet Company's vessels through the Caribbean as a postal service inspector in 1859, described the town as standing "on three hills or mounts, with higher hills, green to their summit, rising behind them. Each mount is topped by a pleasant, cleanly edifice, and pretty looking houses stretch down the sides to the water's edge. . . . As seen from the harbour, the town looks like a panorama exquisitely painted." He went on to describe its citizens much less charitably as comprising a "Hispano-Dano-Niggery-Yankee-doodle population." Trollope saw St. Tomas as a sump, the low point into which things and people drained. "Men who settle at St. Thomas," he sniffed, "have most probably roughed it elsewhere unsuccessfully." He recommended relocating the hub to Jamaica.

The town's lasting allure, however, was not its picturesque, tropical setting, its lush vistas that hinted deceptively at prosperous tobacco and sugar plantations, plantations that during the past century had migrated to more suitable St. Croix instead. The real attraction lay in a superb and well-protected four-hundred-acre harbor made even more comely by its excellent facilities, and an enlightened Danish port administration that attracted ships with low customs charges and cheap transit services. A navigation light installed in 1844 ninety-five feet above sea level atop Muhlenfeldt Point welcomed the surge in shipping that began around midcentury.

The harbor was sheltered from running seas, but its isolation had a serious consequence. Charlotte Amalie's harbor waters were not flushed clean by tidal action, so human waste, garbage, and other pollutants from town and ships at anchor collected in the basin, fouling it. This nasty slurry grew progressively more unpleasant until 1860, when a channel was cut to the open sea in the hope that the pumping action of tides and ocean currents would contribute to cleansing the basin. The remedy was not completely successful, and through the end of the century Charlotte Amalie remained notorious "as a Dutch oven for cooking fever in," in the words of one commentator. Cholera, small-pox, malaria, and yellow fever were all common. Leprosy—dreaded since before medieval times—was also present.

Even so, Charlotte Amalie's geography was compelling, and Royal Navy mail packets from Falmouth, England, had been coming to the port twice a month since 1835. ("Packet" simply described any ship sailing on a fixed schedule.) Before then, civilian sailing packets from Falmouth had visited the port regularly.

Money was swiftly raised, and in 1840 the new Royal Mail company put fourteen identical wood-hulled paddle steamers, each of 1,285 gross tons, on order at seven yards. The cost of this "first fleet," roughly £800,000 (and priced by most shipyards at so many pounds sterling per displacement ton), reflected an expensive Royal Navy requirement that all packets be able to carry heavy deck guns on their weather decks in case of war. Contingency planning was serious: one coal bunker was designed to be convertible to an ammunition magazine for use in the event the ships were pressed into the navy. Going forward, the Royal Navy would retain a substantial, almost paternal interest throughout in everything that the company did, and all its ships had to pass inspection by a Royal Navy surveyor before going to sea. As it would develop, the company's fleet never fired a shot in anger. Some of its vessels, however, were pressed into service hauling troops and military materiel to the Black Sea during the Crimean War. Their sudden diversion threw the mail schedule into chaos for a time.

Royal Mail operations began remarkably quickly, all things considered, after Macqueen presented the idea to Her Majesty's Government in late 1837. An important element in the go-ahead decision might well have been the suggestion by Macqueen—

prediction, as it would turn out—that absent continued British control of routes to the islands, political influence over them might well devolve upon the Americans.

The company's contract, signed in March 1840, required 684,816 miles of steaming in the twelve months between December 1841 and November 1842, a distance equal to almost thirty-two times around the world at the equator. The first year's subsidy was to be a princely £240,000, just over £1 for every three miles steamed—in 1840 one pound sterling represented a London laborer's wages for a seventy-hour week. The subsidy was based on miles steamed, and as the contracted route structure and schedule changed, so too did the payment made. But the government's largess came with heavy penalties for late sailings and missed ports, and heated disputes between ships' masters and their embarked naval agents, and between company management and the Admiralty were commonplace.

Pushed along by single-cylinder, 400-horsepower engines churning fixed wooden paddle wheels, the new company's mail packets were capable of eight or nine knots on open water. (A few years later more efficient feathering floats replaced the fixed floats on paddle wheels and added a knot or two.) Prudently, each ship carried a suit of auxiliary sails, nearly 70,000 square feet of canvas that could be sent up on three masts and their associated yards either to boost speed or to provide propulsion should the engine fail or coal stocks be exhausted. While the specifications for all fourteen were the same, the ships that came off the ways were not. Practices at the yards and some misunderstandings accounted for the differences.

At the insistence of the Royal Navy, thinking about war at sea and still persuaded that familiar wooden hulls could absorb shot better than the new (and brittle) wrought-iron ones, all of the first fourteen ships were built of wood, not metal.[2] Indeed, not until 1852, after RMS *Amazon*, Capt. William Symonds, burned to the waterline at sea that January 4, just two days into her maiden voyage, were the first new-construction, iron-hulled steam packets put on order. (Only 20 or so of the 156 on board *Amazon* survived, among them only a few of the passengers. The others, including all of *Amazon*'s officers, drowned in the desperate effort to launch the ship's boats. The monument to her dead is at St. Michael's Church in Southampton.)

As it turned out, the first departures from—homeport with mail on board were late, but not by much. On January 3, 1842, scheduled mail service began. The complex, interlocking schedule quickly proved itself wildly optimistic (Macqueen's chief error) and had to be amended to reflect the reality of inevitable delays due to many factors.

By 1867 the Royal Mail Steam Packet Company had been operating twice-a-month scheduled service from Southampton, England, to the Caribbean for twenty-five years. Regular service would continue more or less uninterrupted for the next seventy years, until its termination just after World War I, when British resources could no longer sustain a costly subsidy for Caribbean mails.

3

Royal Mail Ship *Rhone*

RMS *Rhone*, 1,700 registered tons, 310 feet long, 40 feet abeam, and drawing just over 25 feet of water, was the sixth screw steamer in service with the company. Illustrations make Rhone look sleek as a seal: bowsprit thrusting eagerly forward, hull free of disfiguring paddle boxes, masts bracketing a painted-black stack tipped rakishly aft.

RMS *Esk*, 231 tons, a diminutive brigantine, was the first vessel in the company's fleet that boasted auxiliary screw propulsion. "Auxiliary" here meaning that the steam engine helped propel the ship, a tentative first step in the transition from familiar sail to promising steam. The next step would reverse the relationship, although these later steamers often had sails aloft even while under power. Not until early in the twentieth century would most steamships go to sea without any sails at all.

Esk first sailed under company colors for Rio de Janeiro and Buenos Aires from Southampton in November 1850, the smallest ship that ever sailed under the RMSP flag. The gentlemen's and ladies' saloons—the sexes' public rooms were kept decorously apart, and these did double duty as passenger berthing spaces—were each not much bigger than a small child's bedroom today. (The incongruous word was borrowed from Victorian usage on land, where "saloon" described the grand room used to receive visitors and guests in a manor house.) This Lilliputian vessel, 112 feet long, with a draft of just 14 feet and Spartan accommodations for twenty-nine passengers and a crew of twenty-two, was sold a few years after her brave first voyage as being unsuitably small to serve even as what the company called an "intercolonial vessel" on feeder routes. Bitter passenger complaints had sped her retirement from the fleet. Evidently *Esk*'s passengers had never experienced, or had happily forgotten, transatlantic travel as it was just a generation or two earlier, when a typical packet's half-dozen "inclosed sleeping-cabins" were each little larger than a coffin: 6 feet long and just 3 or 4 feet wide.

The company's transition from paddle steamers, with their great, vulnerable, and inefficient sidewheels amidships (some pairs more than 40 feet in diameter), to more modern screw steamers such as *Rhone* was a very deliberate one, notwithstanding the fact that the superiority of screw propulsion had been conclusively demonstrated years before. In the spring of 1845 a curious Admiralty had arranged a series of contests between the Royal Navy's screw steamer HMS *Rattler* and its paddle steamer HMS *Alecto*. The most decisive test was a tug-of-war at sea on April 3 under maximum power, when the former handily towed the latter backward at nearly three knots, despite *Alecto*'s twin wheels flailing enthusiastically in the opposite direction.

In retrospect, the attention-getting, head-to-head trials (or in this case, stern-to-stern trials) appear to have been something of a put-up job, because *Rattler* had been used as a propeller test bed for a year or two earlier, and her performance must have been well understood by the time the two rivals were roped together and set off. In fact, the contest was less revealing than it might have appeared to be. Although the ships were said to have engines of nearly equal power, *Rattler*'s engine actually developed more than twice the horsepower of *Alecto*'s, 300 compared to 141. In the end the correct conclusion, that paddle wheels were a technological dead end, was drawn from a flawed analysis.

Even so, the same conservatism that worked to delay adopting iron hulls in place of wooden ones seemingly operated here, too, because it took fifteen years for the next half dozen of the more modern ships to follow *Esk*, and two of those six,

Oneida and *Tasmanian*, joined the fleet almost by accident. They were orphaned by the collapse of their parent European and Australian Royal Mail Company. During those same fifteen years, 1850–65, as if hedging its bet on the new technology, the company continued to introduce wooden-hulled vessels into the fleet, notwithstanding the obvious danger potentially posed by coal fires. The last wooden ship would not be retired until 1871.

Rhone, registered in London as No. 52792, went into scheduled transatlantic mail service on her maiden voyage from England to Brazil October 9, 1865, an unexplained eight months after she was launched in February, with Capt. Robert Woolward in command. Compared to *Esk*, Rhone's accommodations must have been regarded as nearly regal. The trim vessel, moreover, was ideal for long routes: fast (14 knots under steam was demonstrated during sea trials at Stokes Bay in September), comfortable (with 253 first-class accommodations and another 30 each in second and third classes), and even with some space for high-value cargo alongside the dusty bunkers that nearly filled the hold with bagged coal.

Company engineers and procurement agents were very sophisticated about the fuel that drove their ships. Coal quality was carefully rated according to which mine it came from, and even from which particular seam in the mine it came. The "best Welsh" grade, seamen knew, burned almost twice as hot as plain "Staffordshire" coal and the extra heat meant additional range. No one knew more about coal than the British; by the time *Rhone* sailed they had been mining and burning the stuff, and breathing its noxious combustion gases, for more than five hundred years. It was miserable to handle, however—dirty, dusty, and heavy. Coaling ship was a nasty job, and when it was over, everything and everyone anywhere nearby was marked by it, even those idlers who merely stood and watched St. Thomas' native women doing the heavy lifting in baskets atop their heads for one dollar a day.

Mail subsidies and passenger fares are what made the company's business plan work, especially the former. Weight and space limitations meant that freight did not make a big contribution to revenues until late in the century, but the Royal Mail's vessels very often sailed homeward with gold, "naked bar silver," minted coins, and occasionally gemstones and pearls on board in a specially secured bullion room below decks. The record single load might have been worth £1.5 million, an enormous fortune then. The conveyance of this "treasure" without loss ("defalcation" was the crime described in company regulations) and risk of smuggling were the focus of exacting procedures.

Elemental mercury, used in the extraction of gold from ore, was another important cargo during the gold rush years around midcentury, and flasks of quicksilver carefully packed in sawdust and crated often moved outbound on company ships. (On her last voyage in 1845, RMS *Tweed* was carrying 1,115 flasks of mercury for the mines of Mexico as cargo. They became the objects of a special salvage effort.) Occasionally enough of the heavy stuff was carried to affect the trim of the vessels.

Thanks to the Royal Mail, the fastest route from Europe to the gold fields of California for people and small package freight was not the well-known and often thrilling circumnavigation of South America via Cape Horn but through St. Thomas and across the Caribbean and Gulf of Mexico, then by company mule train fifty miles over the isthmus from Colón to Panama City on the Pacific, and finally by ship to San Francisco.[1]

RMS *Rhone*'s fine sea-keeping qualities were confirmed very soon after she first went into service. In January 1866, early in her second passage to Rio, *Rhone* survived "a terrific gale" in the Bay of Biscay. She lost the sheep pens and three ship's boats stored on deck to the winter storm, had two others banged up, and saw two horses killed and one man injured, but little other damage was done. SS *London*, on her third trip to Australia since launching, a year older than Rhone and not far away, sank in the same tempest that doughty Rhone successfully fought off, drowning more than two hundred. *London* is commonly believed to have been badly overloaded and poorly officered.

RMS *Rhone* made six-round trips carrying South American mails between Southampton and Rio de Janeiro, via Lisbon,

Figure 3. "The *Rhone*, One of the Vessels Lost in the Hurricane in the West Indies." *From the* Illustrated London News, *November 28, 1867.*

Madeira, St. Vincent in the Cape Verde Islands (where coal for the leg across to the bulge of Brazil was loaded on board), Pernambuco, and Bahia, before being upgraded to the company's premier, West Indian service in late spring 1867.

In early autumn, on October 2, RMS *Rhone* steamed out of Southampton, England, with a load of passengers, mail, and high-value cargo and headed downriver for distant Charlotte Amalie Harbor, for more than a decade the established center of the Royal Mail's extensive Caribbean operation. This voyage was the nearly new ship's third Atlantic crossing on the West Indian mail schedule. Her first crossing, near the end of May, had taken thirteen days. The second, in late June, took fourteen. On this trip, with Captain Woolley, forty-seven, again in command, *Rhone* made the passage in just twelve days, a full week faster than the pioneering paddle steamers had been able to manage in 1842.

As Macqueen had originally envisioned it, the RMSP's Caribbean hub was to have been at Samaná, Haiti, on the eastern tip of Hispaniola, across the Mona Passage from Puerto Rico. At the time, both islands were Spanish properties. Force majeur, in this case the refusal of the Spanish authorities to cooperate, compelled the temporary relocation of the company's principal Caribbean base to off Turks Island and then to Charlotte Amalie on St. Thomas, one of several changes to the structure of routes first laid out in the "General Plan."

With this stimulation, Charlotte Amalie's port grew rapidly into the company's essential New World hub, offering not only a sheltered anchorage, coaling facilities, and wharves but also (after June 1867) an iron dry dock capable of housing vessels up to 270 feet long and 2,700 tons. The RSMP's very substantial presence on the island accounted for the fact that ashore English was spoken as commonly as Danish, the mother tongue of the island's metropolis.

The usual procedure in 1867 would have been for the arriving steamer from England to tie up to the number 3 buoy in the St. Thomas Harbor, one of two moorings there also known as "hurricane buoys." Once she was in position, intercolonial steamers for the Gulf of Mexico and the Windward Islands would have come up alongside in that order to starboard, and those bound for the harbors of the Spanish Main (the north coast of South America) and Jamaica in that order to port (to "larboard," as the ship's left side was usually called then) to execute the cross-decks exchange of passengers, mail, and cargo.

In the autumn of 1867, however, yellow fever had again forced a new pattern of operation, minimizing the time spent in the now-feverish island capital and in some cases skipping the stop there entirely. Water and victuals were lightered in small boats from St. Croix east to sheltered places in the British Virgin Islands, where reprovisioning could be done under presumably healthier conditions. Coal was floated to the same place in lighters and hulks, dismasted hulls that were commonly used for economical bulk storage afloat, an expensive practice that the frugal Court of Directors would otherwise have wished to avoid. For this reason, Rhone would end this ocean crossing in midmonth near St. Peter's Island, a little more than five miles across the Drake Strait from the island of Tortola and perhaps half a day's cautious steaming from the moribund capital.[2]

J. M. Lloyd, the company's secretary, recorded the situation in the minutes of the April 24, 1867, directors meeting, while strewing commas about in the best nineteenth-century style. "As soon as it was apparent that yellow fever had become epidemic at St Thomas," he wrote:

> the Directors, with a view of keeping the Company's vessels as much as possible out of its influence, issued instructions that the transatlantic ships, which, in the usual course of service, lie a fortnight at St Thomas to coal and prepare for the homeward voyage, should transfer to the Branch ships outside of the Harbour.... With the permission of Her Majesty's Government, they arranged that Peter Island (one of the Virgin Islands), situated about twenty-five miles from St Thomas, and, like the latter, in a central position for the Company's service, should be used temporarily . . . as a place of meeting for all the ships.

4

Riding the *Rhone*

Royal Mail ships were famously well equipped. As Great Britain's mobilization for the Crimean War proved, the Royal Mail's fleet was one of the few at sea in the mid-nineteenth century that fully met the Admiralty's extensive requirements for naval charter without a crash reequipment program. The standard of accommodation and passenger service in *Rhone* was also very high, another point of pride in the company.

Within the limitations of her size and absent electric light and refrigeration (both—coupled with cheap labor—would permit first-class travel by sea to become obscenely opulent in the next century), *Rhone* and her crew treated embarked first-cabin passengers very well indeed. For that reason she was a favorite of oceangoing Victorian gentry and the untitled glitterati of the age.

In addition to a full complement of seamen (meaning deck officers and hands) and engineers, firemen, and coal trimmers, RMSP ships carried a third category of crewmember, servants. This group included cooks, butchers and bakers, stewards, waiters, bootblacks, and all the others whose charge it was to ensure the comfort of the swells on board. There was even a lone female stewardess, with her own cabin aft on the ship's main deck, to care for the special, "delicate" needs of the ladies embarked. Janet Inglis was the stewardess in *Rhone* on this crossing, as she had been on the previous one. All else we know about Inglis is her age, forty-two; her birthplace, Ayroline, Scotland; her pay, a munificent three pounds per month; and the fact that she drowned off Salt Island.

The largest ships on the schedule carried more than twenty servants, one for every ten or so first-class passengers. All were expected to be "orderly, respectful and attentive" to the requirements of their travelers.

In good weather, wealthy passengers could be nearly as comfortable at sea in *Rhone*'s compact but handsome public rooms as they were at home ashore, attended perhaps not only by the well-schooled and deferential stewards of the crew but also by their own familiar household servants, riding the ship on discounted tickets in the second-class cabins below. The all-important mail sacks were stacked in a zinc-lined mailroom in the hold, protected by locks, wire doors, and a seagoing cat specially introduced into the space on every crossing to control the rats that otherwise would devour the bags' leather sides and then foul the mail within them. (A full-time, two-legged professional rat catcher attended the ships when they were in port Southampton to control resident varmints.)

First-class passenger expectations were high. In Victorian England between 5 and 15 percent of the labor force was in domestic service; the proportion increased as the century went on. As might be expected in a society so orderly and class-conscious that it happily took the beehive as its model of social organization, members of the British upper class accepted cosseting by attendants as their due. In the epoch to come, the great passenger liners would boast that their ships' service staffs outnumbered the rest of the crew; on some vessels the number of embarked personal service staff equaled or even exceeded the number of passengers—a balance of servants and the served that is possible to see today only in reruns of *Upstairs, Downstairs* and *Downton Abbey*.

The quality of food service drew the special attention of the company's directors. Like executives in cruise line management today, the directors then understood that thinking about the next meal, actually eating it, and then talking about it afterward could usefully take up a large part of an otherwise empty day at sea. Every saloon galley was staffed with an English *and* a French cook, who could refer to their ship's copy of Soyer's *Cookery Book*, placed on board by the company for passenger menu planning and recipes.[1] Good French cooks were valued so highly by the company that they were paid even while idle ashore in between sailings. When *Rhone* sailed from Southampton for Charlotte Amalie, she had on board five crewmen from France, two cooks, two waiters, and an assistant steward.

Royal Mail vessels on the Brazil route were required to have a good Portuguese cook on board and to offer a selection of national dishes at every meal; the saloon staff included Portuguese-speaking waiters. Descending to a level of detail seen nowhere else in the company's General Regulations, the board directed that to heighten the comfort of its passengers to Brazil, *palitos* (toothpicks made of orange wood, the Regulations explained soberly; the material is splinter free) always be available on the dinner table. The saloon incident that provoked this persnickety written requirement must have been interesting to witness.

Crew messing was not nearly so grand. Board of Trade regulations prescribed in detail the unprepared rations to be served out to the crew by day of the week. For every man, one pound of bread, a pound and a half of meat, an ounce of tea, and two ounces of sugar every day; three-quarters of a pound of flour, half a pint of peas, and two ounces of suet every other day; and one pint of oatmeal a week. At sea, when on salted rations, every man also received half a pint of lime juice and vinegar each week as scurvy prevention.

Passenger cuisine and comfort was one thing. Entertainment during the crossing was something else. Amusement more stimulating than reading, playing board games, or casual chatting must have been difficult to find. Card playing in the saloons was permitted every day but Sunday, when the crew declined to pass out decks. Gambling was always prohibited. Officers, of course, were strictly forbidden to play cards, although why this injunction was enforced—to prevent unprofessional fraternization with the passengers, to avoid the appearance of dissipation, or to preclude idleness—wasn't made clear in the Regulations. Captains were expected to "rigidly enforce" the prohibition.

This primness did not extend to the matter of strong drink. *Rhone* carried generous stocks of wine, distilled spirits, and brewed malt beverages. Only ice was in very limited supply, and so strictly reserved for use in the passenger saloons. Until the invention of industrial refrigeration, the only source of ice in the islands was that cut from New England fresh-water ponds in winter, carefully shipped south, and warehoused in insulated ice houses. Ice purchased in Colón, company regulations noted, was much cheaper than that obtained in St. Thomas.[2]

Not only the passengers but also the crew imbibed regularly, a situation explained by the fact that as late as the end of nineteenth century, drinking almost anything not boiled in advance or generously laced with alcohol still posed a dire threat to health. (The nexus between cholera and a tainted water supply was scientifically established by a London physician, John Snow, in 1855, but popular acceptance of the connection came slowly.) Through that century and well into the next, alcohol was generally thought to have if not medicinal then at least restorative powers.

In fact, *Rhone* made her own fresh water but it was not for drinking. Her boiler heated water into the low-pressure steam that drove the engine, which slowly cranked the propeller shaft. Because hot salt water is one of the most intensely corrosive fluids there is—it would rapidly eat out the inside of the packet's propulsion plant leaving nothing but a perforated ruin behind—only desalinated water would work well in the plant. Early marine steam engines did make steam from salt water, but the practice came at the expense of high maintenance (frequent scraping of the boiler flue tubes to remove mineral scale) and short life.

Even with her first-in-the-fleet surface condenser (it conserved water by recycling some of the spent steam for reuse), *Rhone* consumed fresh water just as she consumed coal. The difference was, she could make boiler feed water through a distillation process but had to load coal. Only in St. Thomas, where fresh water was in chronically short supply, was boiler feed water diverted for human consumption, and then only in cooking.

To the distress of the temperance movement, alcoholic drinks were a part of the daily ration of most workers, from young scullery maids in households ashore to salty deckhands aloft. A combination beverage, medical tonic, and reward for hard labor. Armies marched and navies floated on the stuff, and even small children drank hard cider and mild ale.

In this, as in everything else on board an RMSP vessel, rank had its privileges. The captain was allowed one full bottle of four-shilling wine per day. Junior deck officers were allowed half as much but could purchase another pint if they wished. Engineer officers got their wine, too, but also received one bottle of beer each day, compensation perhaps for the hellish heat below decks in which these men did their work. If they chose to, all seven engineer officers, from the chief (John Hooper, forty-nine) to the junior engineer (George Ogbun, twenty-two and on his first cruise), could exchange their effete daily pint of wine for a more manly half-pint ration of brandy to accompany the beer. On days that steam was up, lowly firemen and coal trimmers received an extra half gill (a little more than two fluid ounces, or a generous double shot) of rum in addition to the usual gill.

In first-class cabins and below decks, enough was drunk on each crossing that empty bottles represented a measurable economic factor to the company, and its regulations provided that empties were to be carefully stored at sea and returned to port for recycling.

Almost three years after the hurricane in the spring of 1870, when Jeremiah Murphy in his diving dress was bravely and cautiously picking his way through the wreck of the *Rhone* ten fathoms under, he came upon the remains of the ship's spirit room during a dive. Later, on the surface above the wreck and over a lamb dinner, Murphy and his guests sampled cool bottles of champagne, brandy, beer, lemonade, soda, and seltzer water stocked for the return crossing to Southampton that never happened. They judged it all as good as new. According to an account of the repast in the *Port of Spain Gazette*, Murphy's lamb must have been well lubricated. Lacking any champagne flutes to drink from, the party happily quaffed the sparkling salvage from water tumblers.

5

Safety at Sea

The first company packet, Royal Mail Ship *Clyde*—all the company's ships were named after rivers—went into the water in February 1841. Fittingly she was named after the eponymous river in Scotland, site of one of the great incubators of the industrial revolution during a century of extraordinary Scottish brilliance. (That century can be counted to have begun with James Watt in his maturity, say, 1750, and hit the halfway mark in 1801, when William Symington's homely steam tug *Charlotte Dundas* went into the water on the Forth and Clyde Canal.) For a while, much of the world's shipping at sea was built in yards lined along thirty miles of this river's banks between the city of Glasgow and the coast. Favored shipyards on the Clyde would eventually be the source of many of the company's ships.

The company's early record revealed that its was a bold, pioneering enterprise—both adjectives here being euphemisms for risky. The first RMSP ship lost at sea was RMS *Medina*, grounded in May 1842 on Turks Island in the Bahamas; mercifully all 168 on board survived. Between 1841, when scheduled service began, and 1865, when RMS *Rhone* sailed to Rio de Janeiro for the first time in revenue service, the line lost fully thirteen vessels to groundings and storms, more than one every other year. The total included six of the first fourteen ships delivered. Two (*Amazon* and *Parramatta*) sank on their maiden voyages.

Remarkably, one ship beat even that lugubrious record: Even before her maiden voyage, *Demerara* was damaged nearly beyond repair while under tow down the Avon River en route to have her engines installed. The victim of a grotesquely inept tow, *Demerara* remained unlucky throughout. Eventually rebuilt as a sailing ship and renamed *British Empire*, she sailed as a collier to St. Thomas in October 1867, and with 3,800 tons of coal on board was one of the many ships sunk by the hurricane at the end of the month. (She was raised in August 1868.)

High seas and storm winds, poor charts and limited navigation aids, inept seamanship, greedy owners overloading their vessels, and incendiary cargoes and materials on board— each was responsible for some part of a record that amassed horrific losses at sea as the nineteenth century unfolded. Fire was an especially fearful ship killer. "On a hot, dry night, especially in the tropics," one author wrote, "a sailing ship moved as a sort of tinderbox, all its standing rigging covered with tar, its deck seams caulked with tar, and much of its dry woodwork heavily coated in either oil-based paint or linseed oil mixed with tar." But so, too, was foul weather. By late in the century, a typical year in the North Atlantic might see one hundred or more steamships founder in high seas and storm winds, just as *London* had in the Bay of Biscay.

Until regulations post–RMS *Titanic* forced a common and more solicitous approach to lifesaving on the high seas, shipping company management was generally free to define its own response to emergencies and to equip its ships accordingly. Some lines, Cunard was representative of these, were famously skeptical about the utility of onboard lifesaving equipment and cavalier about risk. A very few others, the Royal Mail among them, were much more considerate and insisted on space in a lifeboat for everyone on board the ship.

Meteorology had progressed to an awkward point in the 1850s and 1860s: Weather was thought to be predictable, but forecasting wasn't yet possible. Pioneers of "meteorological philosophy" in the United Kingdom, Adm. Francis Beaufort and Adm. Robert FitzRoy chief among them, were moving past simple sailors' and farmers' aphorisms drawn from biblical verse into the beginnings of a real science of forecasting, but for decades still to come foul weather would arrive on the scene literally as a bolt from the blue. The deadly San Narciso hurricane of late October 1867 hit the Virgins like that.

"Looking at the destructive character of these storms," the *London Daily News* wrote that November 9, in the aftermath of the hurricane,

> their terrible frequency, and the importance of the navigation which has its track in the region where they spend their fury, it is natural to ask whether we may not hope that our present helpless subjugation to their power will one day disappear. It seems that all we can reasonably expect is to become better acquainted with the condition of their recurrence, and be able to take warning by the signs which herald their approach. Even these wild tumults of the elements, as we imagine them, have their laws, which we are gradually coming to understand. The subject has received much elucidation during the last twenty years. . . . Our seamen are now in possession of a body of practical information as to the way of avoiding hurricanes and managing ships in them, which will prove useful in saving lives and property. But when all has been done, the navigation of these seas from August to the end of October will remain a service of peril.

The paper's sober view of the progress of science came immediately after a paragraph of unintentional fiction, describing a storm so violent that it "forced the Gulf Stream back to its source, and piled up the water in the Gulf of Mexico to the height of thirty feet so that [a ship] that attempted to ride the storm out, found herself when it had abated, high up on the dry land, and discovered that she had let go her anchor among the tree tops."

Not until more than a century after FitzRoy, when the required instantaneous communications, specialized sensors, computer processors, complex algorithms, and satellite observation finally fell into place, did meteorological philosophy become modern science. In the meanwhile, as late as the start of the twentieth century it was possible for a killer storm hundreds of miles in diameter to arrive as a complete surprise—as one did at Galveston, Texas, in 1900—and run up on shore to drown thousands. Not until 1909 did a ship first alert those on land of weather coming from seaward.

RMSP ships sailed with British Admiralty charts for navigation, and by the 1860s for the most traveled routes these charts were really quite good, although not perfect as occasional groundings on misplotted or missed entirely reefs demonstrated. (The deadly collision of the submarine USS *San Francisco* with an uncharted seamount in the Pacific Ocean in January 2005 confirms that perfect charts have continued to elude mariners.) Users of any other charts were warned by company directors "to be on their guard against errors which may prove fatal"— always good advice. The company augmented available charts with a book of sailing directions and with cautions it published in its Regulations and in circular letters. Given the apparent ubiquity of reefs, groundings merited a special warning:

> If in spite of all the cautions given, any of the Company's ships should hereafter be run on shore, the order to reverse engines, or to *back her*, is never to be given, till from examination it can be ascertained, that the damage done to the ship's bottom is likely not to occasion foundering after she is floated. Had this precaution been taken on board the steamers "Solway" and "Victoria," hundreds of lives might have been saved.

Business losses, the costs to investors and entrepreneurs of the ships and cargoes that sailed only to never reappear in port, had been considered ages earlier. At the end of the sixteenth century, landsman William Shakespeare was writing brilliantly about tempests that destroyed fleets and threw castaways ashore, and about the terrible "peril of waters, winds and rocks." Shakespeare's "tempest" was the great Bermuda hurricane of 1609. That storm caught a fleet of settlers from England bound for Virginia near midocean. Some ships managed to reach the island, presumably including the one carrying Prospero and Miranda, who first appeared on stage in 1611. And Venetian merchant Antonio's huge and uninsured losses at sea—argosies bound for Tripoli, for the Indies, Mexico, and England, which one after another failed to arrive—made it impossible for him to repay his debt to Shylock in *The Merchant of Venice*. The disappearance of Antonio's ships, deep-draft merchantmen built in the Sicilian style, not only ruined him financially but also, thanks to the Jewish moneylender's flinty determination to collect his bond, condemned him to death.[1]

In 1696, a century after Shakespeare wrote *The Merchant of Venice*, Edward Lloyd started publishing a list of ship movements that he made available to patrons of his coffeehouse near the Thames River docks. From that inspired journalism eventually came the Society of Lloyds and the modern marine insurance industry. By the beginning of the nineteenth century, seafaring countries were host to more or less workable insurance schemes that shielded shipowners and shippers not only from such theatric liability as Antonio's but also from the worst economic consequences of random loss.

Almost since the company's beginning, however, Royal Mail ships sailed without commercial insurance once they left Southampton on their maiden voyage. Ships were insured only while under construction and in homeport (years after the fact the company was finally able to collect from its underwriters for the loss of *Demerara*) but not while on the high seas and in port abroad. Because of the large premiums required to cover these risks in the commercial market, 8 percent and higher said the company's centennial historian, these latter risks were self-insured and the company booked a reserve fund for this purpose. This policy meant that after the storm in 1867, the total cost of replacement of three vessels, the repair of three badly damaged ones, and the restoration of its battered shoreside facilities was entirely to the company's account. Such self-insurance was possible in the era before claims for loss of life and companionship and for "pain and suffering" incurred became expensive features of post-accident litigation.

Passenger traffic on the high seas exploded in the nineteenth century, pushed by dreadful conditions at home, pulled by the lure of cheap farmland and a fresh start overseas, and lubricated by low-cost steerage fares that made intercontinental travel possible even by refugees. One result was great loss of life. Ships foundered and passengers drowned in big numbers throughout the century, statistics absorbed with astonishing stoicism. By the standards of the day, the Royal Mail's record wasn't remarkable at all.

6

The Royal Mail Steam
Packet Company in Operation

Despite what to modern eyes looks like a disconcerting record of lost lives and destroyed property, for its first forty-five years the Royal Mail Steam Packet Company was clearly a well-run and well-regulated operation.[1] In part that distinction came from the company's close connection to the Royal Navy, and in part it came from the orderly tendencies of the prudent businessmen who sat on its Court of Directors, as its governing board was styled.

The tie to the Royal Navy had its origin in the fact that the mails being carried after 1842 by company vessels had for nearly twenty years been transported in navy gun brigs, and because mail carriage now was government business under government contract. All RMSP vessels were built to plans approved by the Royal Navy and included structural provisions for their quick conversion to duty as armed auxiliaries. Their clean, stout weather decks were unobstructed—clear of the deck houses that could have contained accommodations or public spaces—so that in case of need, the long gun carriages of nineteenth-century war at sea could be easily emplaced on them.

The Royal Navy representative on board every company vessel at sea (its "Naval Agent," usually a lieutenant with doubtful career prospects) had some powers and perquisites that exceeded her captain's, and many of ship's company officers embarked had prior navy service.

From the beginning the ranks of company personnel ashore and at sea were shot through with serving and retired navy men. The company's first marine superintendent was a certain Lieutenant Kendall, and fully five of the captains taking first fleet company ships out on their maiden voyages in 1841–43 were active duty Royal Navy officers. In midcentury one of the company's three superintendents overseas, the senior executives on scene in the Caribbean and Brazil, was a serving Royal Navy captain. In 1867 two of the eleven members of the company's Court of Directors were retired rear admirals of the Royal Navy.

The close relationship chafed badly sometimes, as the Court of Directors had known it would. Southampton was selected by them as the company's homeport in part because two other choices, nearby Portsmouth and Plymouth, were staunch navy towns, saturated with that service's weighty customs, traditions, and style. A commercial mail packet operation, the Falmouth Postal Packet Service, had operated from Falmouth, England, to the Mediterranean, West Indies, and Brazil from late in the seventeenth century until 1823, when the Admiralty began to take over the routes with Royal Navy brigs. Ten years later the substitution was almost complete.

Throughout the early years of the RMSP, Falmouth's seafarers optimistically predicted the failure of the Southampton-based steamers, hoping to turn back the clock to their own glory days of carrying the mail overseas. Falmouth's newspaper, the *Falmouth Packet and Cornish Herald*, fighting a rear-guard action as late as the 1840s, missed no chance to denigrate steamer service, reliability, and seamanship or to abuse RMSP's management, but the city's distance from London and the lack of a rail connection to the capital made its case for turning back the clock unpersuasive.

Company management on at least one occasion ruefully observed that all its ships commanded by former Royal Navy captains had been run aground and believed that Merchant Service masters were much more interested in commercial matters and passenger well-being. Even so, company ships and crews *looked* smartly naval. Fourteen different uniforms, depending on the grade and employment of the wearer, were prescribed in the Regulations. The many distinctions in cut, material, number and style of buttons, and chevrons of gold lace, braid, or black silk emphasized the hierarchical nature of the organization. (Each instance of uniform violation in port or at sea was to be reported to the company secretary in Southampton, an indication of how seriously the company took its uniform code.) The appearance of company ships was no less carefully defined. Flat white–, drab- (brown), black-, or straw-colored paint was prescribed for certain surfaces; others were to be left unpainted maple or oak but varnished every six months.

In July 1860 the company issued its updated set of General Regulations, a handsome printed volume of almost three hundred pages that replaced all prior instructions, circular letters, and orders. The General Regulations left very little unsaid or to chance, but when necessary its provisions could be supplemented by numbered circular letters, effective until the next edition of the Regulations was published. The 1860 issue was the effective edition under which *Rhone* sailed to the Caribbean in 1867. It was published roughly twenty years after the superseded edition and would be replaced, in turn, about twenty years in the future.

The table of contents of the General Regulations of 1860 hints at the broad scope of concerns held by the Court of Directors. Fully thirty subjects, running through the alphabet from "Admiralty Agents and Mails" to "War Circular," appear in the contents.

No subject, not even seamanship in destructive weather ("Hurricane Months"), took more room in these regulations than did the twenty-seven articles that addressed the "Conveyance of Treasure." The safe transport of precious cargo was the responsibility of the captain, but from receipt to delivery, its supervision and security were practically the full-time business of his crew's third officer, occasionally assisted by the fourth. Even so, the company experienced "heavy losses," especially from shipments from Colón, Panama, and Tampico, Mexico, where special scales were maintained in the effort to ensure honest weight and count of loaded treasure. The pressure on the third officer, a young man in his twenties, liable to the company for any monetary loss and earning all of four pounds per month while at sea (less than his captain's monthly wine allowance), must have been tremendous.

Offloading of treasure at Southampton, England, was no less carefully supervised than loading it abroad. Regulations prescribed that all six ship's officers, including of course the captain, and three other company employees form a chain of custody from the ship's bullion room to the storekeeper ashore. Each participant had a prescribed place to stand and role to play in the transfer.

7

The Virgin Islands

In mid-October 1493 and three weeks out of Spain, the caravel *Nina* stood out of the Canary Islands as part of a flotilla of seventeen vessels that had spent the first half of the month there undergoing repairs, revictualing, and taking on fresh water before braving the three-week Atlantic crossing westbound. On this, his second voyage to the New World, Christopher Columbus was traveling with a fleet more appropriate to his status as "admiral of the ocean sea" than the hastily assembled trio of his first voyage, the unhandy carrack *Santa Maria* and her two tiny consorts. More than one thousand, perhaps as many as fifteen hundred men and a few women, were embarked in his great fleet on its great adventure. Fifteen square-rigged ships, two with the triangular lateen sails that lent them an exotic, Mediterranean look.

Somewhere on board one or more of the ships was a small stock of green cargo, sugar-cane cuttings from Spain's Madeira Islands in the eastern Atlantic, where cane was now the basis of an important business. It would develop that sugar cane, having migrated westward from New Guinea across the ages, would grow wonderfully well in the New World, in Brazil, and on the islands. In full sun and with ample water, individual stalks could rise in over a year to fifteen or sixteen feet high, as stout, reports one account, as a man's wrist. From lush new fields and enormous labor would come enough sugar eventually to make what had once been a spice and medicine reserved for the wealthy into a food for the working class. But that transformation came at a terrible price. Not ten years after sugar landed in the new world, so did the first African slaves.

The admiral's intention this time was to approach his destination from the southeast. The navigation technology of the day required sailing along parallels of latitude, but ships' masters had no way of fixing their position east or west on these imaginary lines and could only guess at it through crude estimates of speed and distance made good. Pushed along briskly by reliable easterlies, Columbus's fleet made its first landfall at Maria Galante in today's Windward Islands. During the next six months, the fleet would slowly sail almost to the western tip of Cuba, hemstitching through the Antilles sometimes on the Atlantic side and sometimes on the Caribbean before finally turning about to depart the archipelago through a passage in the Leeward Islands and heading back to Cadiz, where all arrived in June 1494.

Early on, in mid-November 1493 out of St. Martín and while bound for (without knowing it) Samaná Bay on Hispaniola, the Spanish fleet passed Santa Cruz, now St. Croix, and the rest of the Virgin Islands far off to starboard. Columbus named the small cluster of islands on the horizon after the martyr St. Ursula, slain in Cologne during the third century AD for her faith. She died in the company of as few as five or as many as eleven thousand virgin martyrs (the number depending on how one read the inscription in a church choir that described her sacrifice and one's level of credulity). And so it was that the Virgin Islands, small bits of land spangled across the eastern entrance to what soon became the Spanish Main, were introduced to the Old World.

Nothing east of Puerto Rico was big enough to hold Spanish attention. Spain's focus elsewhere (on the riches of Central and South America, on Puerto Rico and Cuba, Florida and California), left the Antilles, including the Virgins, open to her competitors—the Dutch, French, English, and Danes, among others—who saw opportunity in the exotic products of tropical agriculture, if only a way were found to keep a labor force productive in the face of disease. That way turned out to be the slave trade, which efficiently and heartlessly, but not illegally, simply replenished the inventory as it died off. Before it was finally outlawed and arrested, this cruel business brought as many as 12 million blacks from Africa to labor, suffer, and die on the plantations and in the mines of the Americas.

In 1733 the Copenhagen-based West India and Guinea Company purchased St. Croix from the French, renaming it Sankt Croix and adding this third island to Sankt Thomas and Sankt Jan, the existing Danish colonies in the Dansk Vestindien, the Danish West Indies. Twenty years later, the pretty islands, the site of lush sugar plantations and home to fevers so lethal that they practically chased Europeans back where they came from, became the property of the Danish crown. They remained so until finally sold to the United States in 1917 for $25 million. As U.S. territories, the islands formed part of the outer defenses of the Panama Canal, and for this reason they were governed by navy officers until 1931.

The Caribbean became important to Great Britain as a geographic extension of wars in Europe, and especially so while British interests in the New World grew in parallel with the empire's North American colonies. The focus of that interest fell on the Leeward Islands, on Antigua, Barbados, and Jamaica, but the fact that the Virgins lay along the efficient sailing track into the Gulf of Mexico guaranteed their importance.

In 1493 it took Columbus some seven weeks to make his Atlantic crossing to the Virgin Islands; three and a half centuries later, *Rhone* would manage it in fewer than two. Both voyages were done at roughly the same time of year, near the tail end of the hurricane season in the western Atlantic and Caribbean.

8

The Yellow Fever Epidemic of 1867

"They cannot understand at home why we dislike the inter-colonial work so much," a Royal Mail captain told Anthony Trollope during the latter's inspection tour in 1858–59. "They do not comprehend at home what it is for a man to be burying one young officer after another; to have them sent out, and then to see them mown down in that accursed hole of a harbour by yellow fever." Trollope then explained the conversation to readers of his travelogue and further pressed his case against Charlotte Amalie:

> These captains themselves and their senior officers are doubtless acclimated. The yellow fever may reach them but their chance of escape is tolerably good; but the young lads who join the service, and do so at an early age, have at the first commencement of their career to make St. Thomas their residence, as far as they have any residence. They live of course on board their ships; but the peculiarity of St. Thomas is this; that the harbour is ten times more fatal than the town. It is that hole, up by the coaling wharves, which sends so many English lads to the grave.

Trollope's campaign against the Danish island capital was initially unsuccessful. Years after his inspection tour, the RMSP's transatlantic packet schedule still provided for a two-week layover at this terminal and coaling station in the eastern Caribbean before returning to England—and it continued to even after RMS *Tasmanian*, Capt. E. M. Leeds, arrived at Southampton in mid-December 1866 from St. Thomas with seventy-one cases of fever among the crew on board, twenty-five of them fatal.

Yellow fever—the disease is incurable even today—struck especially hard the following autumn across the Antilles Islands and the Caribbean Sea and through the Gulf of Mexico, spanning an ocean area of nearly 2 million square miles, latitude 15°, longitude 40°. Every settlement washed by these waters was vulnerable. At Fort Jefferson, the grim U.S. federal prison on Dry Tortugas in the Florida Keys, yellow fever from Cuba killed one of the four jailed Lincoln assassination conspirators and left another (physician Samuel Mudd, he who set the assassin Booth's broken leg), the only doctor alive on the island, to treat the diseased. At the other end of the gulf the "dread calamity" sharply thinned the population of Corpus Christi, Texas, forcing its *Office Advertiser* that August to publish grim rosters of its small city's dead. To the north, Galveston's bout in 1867 was the ninth time the coastal Texas city had been struck by the disease in twenty-eight years.

As *Rhone* approached Charlotte Amalie on October 14, the harbor was uncharacteristically quiet. The noisy school of small cutters and bum boats that usually put out from the town across sapphire water—hawking fruit and other foodstuffs, trying to sell rides to shore, or just sharing in the excitement of greeting a visitor—to welcome every arrival from overseas was quiescent. That's because in the two months since *Rhone*'s departure from the island on August 16, life in the waterfront capital had been overwhelmed by yellow fever.

Warned away by the homeward-bound paddle steamer RMS *Atrato* when twelve miles off Charlotte Amalie, Woolley wisely steamed on. He went northeast some thirty miles toward Road Town, on Tortola Island. Near there, south of Round Bay and across the strait, tucked in cozily off St. Peter's Island's Great Harbor, Woolley began to unload his ship and prepare for the return voyage. Such diversions to preserve crew and passenger health were thought to be worth the "considerable extra expense" and "unavoidable delay" they imposed.

In the three centuries before yellow fever was conquered in 1900, time ashore in the Caribbean (or on Bermuda) was

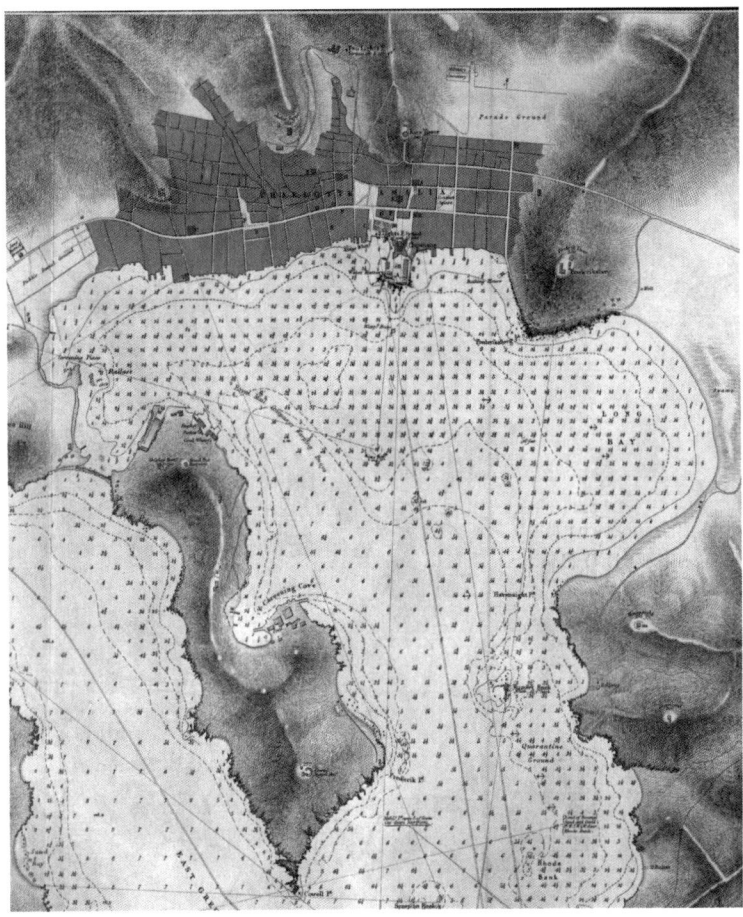

Figure 4. "Harbour of St. Thomas. The RMSP Company's coaling wharves lay southwest of Christians Fort and the water battery, near the heart of Charlotte Amalie's inner harbor, and beneath the 215' peak on which stood the small pox hospital and the ruins of Shipley Battery, destroyed in the island's last great hurricane. The company's warping buoys, where mail and passenger exchanges usually took place, bobbed less than one-quarter mile offshore. Detail from British Admiralty Chart No. 2183 (1853)." *Library of Congress.*

often tantamount to a death sentence, especially to British army regiments posted to the theater. Such "wastage" due to fatal disease occasionally resulted in the unit's dissolution, requiring its replacement to be recruited anew. Royal Navy losses were somewhat fewer, but even so one-quarter to one-third of a ship's crew was expected to be "wasted," dead and buried at sea or completely incapacitated, during a single cruise in these waters.

The disease originally came from Africa. It traveled west in the transatlantic vessels that plied this increasingly busy route between continents, in the fresh-water casks down in the holds or perhaps in the bloodstreams of their crews. Exactly when yellow fever arrived in the New World isn't known, but the first recorded epidemic of the disease seems to have happened just before the mid-seventeenth century, when it erupted in Barbados in 1647. During the next several years, yellow fever appeared in most Caribbean and Gulf Coast ports and in Atlantic Florida. By the late 1860s, yellow fever was both dreadful and familiar throughout the Caribbean.

The name alone was frightening to initiates. Its course was terrible: "Lassitude, glazed eyes, chills, fevers, headaches, nausea, retching, and nose bleeds would suddenly attack people in the best of health. These symptoms, more violent than any the doctors had ever observed, would be followed by a yellow tinge in the eyeballs, puking, fearful straining of the stomach, the black vomit, hiccoughs, depression, 'deep and distressed sighing, comatose delirium,' stupor, purplish discoloration of the whole body, finally death." Sometimes all of that in just hours from start to finish. In some places yellow fever killed 20 to 30 percent of all those infected. On board *Tasmanian* in late 1866, the case fatality rate approached 40 percent.

Yellow fever was very familiar to Americans, too, and not just to those who lived along the Gulf Coast. An epidemic in Philadelphia in 1793, carried into what was then the United States' largest city and national capital by refugees from Santo Domingo, brought home almost to New England how terrible this disease was. Yellow fever literally decimated the city, killing 10 percent of its residents, shutting down national

Figure 5. "The Town and Harbour of St. Thomas, West Indies, the Scene of the Recent Destructive Hurricane." *From the* Illustrated London News, *November 16, 1867.*

and state government, and chasing many fearful citizens out of Philadelphia in search of refuge. Other outbreaks of the virus dotted the New England coast and struck at Nantucket, and at least once got as far north as Halifax, Nova Scotia. Depending on the source of the data and the place described, the mysterious epidemic seemed to reoccur every several years.

Generations later, during the last year of the Civil War, Washington seethed with rumors that cunning, cruel rebels were shipping infected clothing into the city, hoping to trigger a yellow fever epidemic that could reverse the course of the war. (That form of germ warfare would have worked with smallpox, but vector-borne yellow fever couldn't be transmitted in this way.)

Just after that war some claimed to find good in yellow fever. A callous *New York Times* correspondent writing in Richmond, Virginia, on the last day of October 1867, allowed as how the "twin plagues" of yellow fever and the Negro franchise would eventually force a salutary population redistribution in the newly reunited country, thus solving "the negro question," which, evidently, the Civil War had left unresolved. Under pressure from yellow fever's "fearful ravages" in the South during 1867, those of Saxon and German blood would relocate to the healthy and industrious North, he thought. Meanwhile, "Latins, Ethiopians, and embrowned Indians," all believed immune to the disease, would cluster "within the charmed circle of perennial Summer, which is swept by cyclones, hurricanes and that avenging cruiser Bronze John (or Yellow Jack)."

The belief that Africans, natives of yellow fever's home continent, were immune to the disease was commonplace. When Captain Woolward's first command, *Great Western*, was struck with yellow fever in the 1850s, he promptly paid off his white crew and shipped a crew of black replacements, "after which I had no more yellow fever troubles." The exchange left only Woolward, his chief officer, and a single midshipman on board from the original crew, all three presumably also immune—or big risk takers.

Sometime in mid-October, at nearly the same time as *Rhone* dropped anchor in Great Harbor, a weak low-pressure area formed over the dunes of the African Sahel. Pushed by winds aloft, the low started drifting slowly west from this sere strip of continent. Several days later, and then off the coast of West Africa, the same once-arid, dust-laden warm air mass had grown into a tropical depression, a cluster of thunderstorms moving together across the mid–Atlantic Ocean, sucking their energy from the near 80° F water beneath them. Perhaps even as late as October 22 and 23, when RMS *Rhone* was approaching the midpoint of her turnaround at St. Peter's Island, the slow, general circulation of weather around this central low would have been imperceptible to any ships sailing through it in coastwise trade between Europe and Africa. They would have experienced the nascent system only as individual intermittent, strong squalls.

Such Cape Verde–type hurricanes are unusual after the first half of October. Late October hurricanes tend to develop fully much farther west than do those earlier in the season, deepening and strengthening late in their approach to the Leeward Islands.

9

"Sudden and Imminent Peril"

Hurricanes were the subject of six pages in the RMSP's General Regulations of 1860, and a quotation of an 1848 memorandum by the governor of Barbados added two pages more to the exposition. This extensive text, the directors explained almost apologetically, was offered "not with an intention to convey the least doubt of [captains' and other officers'] professional caution and skill, or to fetter the exercise of their judgment in any respect, but merely to attract attention to matters involving the security of the Company's ships, and the safety of all on board, at a period when they may be subject to sudden and imminent peril." In the Regulations hurricane season was identified as August, September, and October, with the possibility of storms in late July and early November acknowledged.

The modern season in the Atlantic runs from the beginning of June through the end of November. Early and late season tropical cyclones typically rise in the western Caribbean and Gulf of Mexico. Midseason hurricanes usually have a different source, forming along the easterly waves that frequently push off from West Africa over the ocean. Late season hurricanes are usually unrelated to easterly waves. They commonly spin up on the tail end of frontal systems.

Historically, peak activity occurs in the eastern Caribbean during the first half of September; the ninth is the big day statistically. October is the last active month of the annual hurricane season in the eastern Caribbean, but big storms are not uncommon then. Fully one-fifth of all hurricanes during the past five centuries have appeared in October, and several of the worst storms in recorded history—including the great killer of 1780, history's most lethal—came during that month.

In 1867, other than evacuating waterfront structures and fleeing to higher ground, there wasn't much that island residents could have done to prepare themselves for a hurricane, even if they had warning. Ships in port or at anchorages, however, could have put out to sea, to take their chances with the wind and waves rather than risk being "embayed on a lee shore," driven aground. But at the end of October 1867, few had any reason to expect a hurricane so late in the year, and no one ashore or afloat was prepared for one as the barometer began to drop and high clouds finally moved in from the east ahead of landfall. The absence of a general sortie from port and the great number of ships soon to be trapped in the storm suggests that no captain read the clues in the weather any better than did Woolley. Until too late they all missed the true significance of the suddenly falling barometer, growing seas, rainfall, and rising wind. So too, apparently, did Superintendent John Cameron, the company's senior man ashore in the islands and its responsible official at the roadstead. The absence of evident alarm on the part of Cameron and Woolley might have sedated all the others.

The approach of a hurricane was signaled, the Regulations said, by the barometer, and captains were required to have an officer record and report barometric pressure changes to them every hour day and night. An attentive crew might have noticed a falling barometer as much as thirty-six hours ahead of the storm. Even an inattentive one would certainly have noticed it by twenty-four hours out.

Crews were further cautioned that during hurricane season, "whether a barometer indicates evil or not . . . a ship should be kept as snug as possible, particularly between sunset and sunrise." In view of *Rhone*'s plight to come, the Regulations' other specific "observations" about hurricanes are instructive:

Having reason to apprehend the approach of a hurricane, the first object should be to *get clear of land*, so as to obtain ample sea-room for drifting. . . . Having good sea-room, sails furled, yards and gaffs lowered, masts struck, funnels additionally secured, quarter boats on deck and lashed, dead lights, scuttles, and ports shut and thoroughly fastened, hatches on and ready for battening, pumps prepared, &c., &c., . . . In the event of being caught by a hurricane . . . it may be advisable to stop the engines, bank up the fires, spread a few yards of canvas abaft, and heave to, till the fury of the storm subsides. . . . If a ship should encounter a hurricane and find it impossible to clear the land, the steam is always to be kept up ready to take advantage of a lull or shift of wind, or to sheer clear of any drifting ship.

According to a NOAA reconstruction, during the 1867 hurricane season nine storms blew through the western Atlantic, Caribbean, and Gulf of Mexico. The first of these, in late June of the year, made landfall midway up the South Carolina coast and slowly rained itself out as it passed through North Carolina and Virginia. Several others swept along great offshore arcs past the Atlantic seaboard, heading northeast, eventually to die in the high latitudes as cold water sapped their strength. The season's seventh big blow, an early October category 2 hurricane (as measured on today's Saffir-Simpson Hurricane Wind Scale), rose in the Gulf of Mexico, probably along what was left of a stalled, low-pressure frontal trough. It first battered the Texas shore and then flooded waterfront settlements in three other states along the Gulf Coast before crossing over northern Florida and heading out to sea. (Galveston Island suffered painfully from hurricanes again. In early September 1900, a great storm drowned the city, killing perhaps as many as 12,000 citizens. Galveston recovered slowly, but for evermore the once-proud East Texas port city took second place to nearby Houston.)

The year's ninth and last storm, the San Narciso hurricane of October 27–31, was by far the season's worst.[1] This was a category 3 storm, and it fell from the sky onto the Virgin Islands like a bomb.

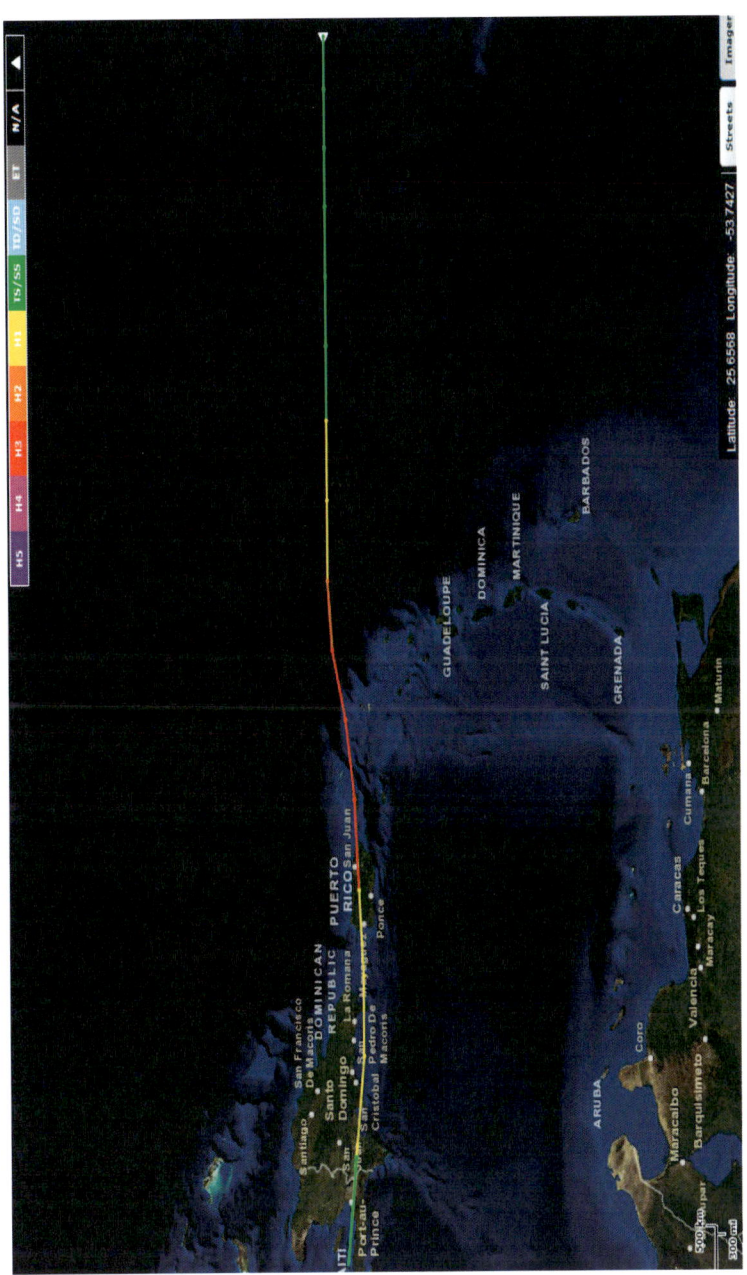

Figure 6. The 1867 hurricane season, from a National Oceanic and Atmospheric Administration North Atlantic hurricane tracking chart. *NOAA*

San Narciso first appeared in the western Atlantic in tropical storm strength, with all the appurtenances of an infant cyclone—bands of rain spiraling out from its center, embedded thunderstorms, and winds churning at just over forty knots—when it crossed 50° west longitude at sunrise on Sunday, October 27. Steered by the prevailing easterlies, and with its thunderstorms already grown to towering height in the absence of stratospheric westerlies that could have shorn off their tops, the storm had followed almost exactly the traditional ocean-crossing route of nineteenth-century sailing vessels south of the Bermuda high-pressure dome, growing more coherent as it progressed. That evening, the storm began to intensify. Wind speeds probably increased at the maximum rate, by about thirty knots in every twenty-four-hour period, spinning ever more powerfully around a developing central eye until they peaked late Tuesday, October 29.

In the last four days of October, San Narciso continued to track almost due west down a line roughly along 19° north latitude at an average speed of fourteen knots. Its course took the strengthening storm directly atop the Virgin Islands and Puerto Rico.

During the critical twenty-four-hour period while what had by then become a hurricane visited the Virgin Islands and Puerto Rico, from late Tuesday evening, October 28, to the same time the next day, San Narciso suddenly grew into a behemoth. In this terrific form the juggernaut rolled over the islands and overhead RMS *Rhone*. At maximum strength when San Narciso impaled the Virgins, around 6:00 p.m. local time October 29, storm winds blew around its eye wall at 110 knots, more than 125 miles per hour. Gusts would have been stronger.

As the hurricane's eye passed overhead, atmospheric pressure dropped to 27.95 inches, almost 2 inches below normal. The low pressure at the heart of the cyclone actually sucked the surrounding ocean up into a mound, imperceptible to sailors at sea, raising local sea level a foot or two above the surrounding waters. When San Narciso ran over shallow water approaching shore, however, its storm surge topped out at ten to twelve feet, the additional height coming from onshore winds pushing up the sea. Beginning hours before the arrival of the eye and lasting until well after its departure, low-lying terrain, anything below ten feet or so above sea level, was flooded far inland by the surge.

San Narciso's late development and speed of advance robbed Woolley and his fellow captains of the usual weather warnings as the hurricane closed in. Typically such a storm would have been heralded not only by barometric change but also by rising seas and freshening winds, by progressively lower cloud cover, by intermittent showers, and then by torrential rain beginning thirty-six hours or more in advance. Instead, San Narciso's small size and late development likely produced only a very small convective cloud shield, delaying the appearance of the usual harbingers of trouble.

So it was that just in front of the storm, even as the hurricane began to move under high pressure aloft, a warm autumn sun beat down reassuringly (if falsely) through generally blue skies. On St. Thomas October 27, before a sudden change in the weather at "12 ¼ o'clock p.m.," a single morning shower seems to have been the only blemish on what started as a fine day. Surprise everywhere was complete. Even after a sudden northwest gale brought torrential rains just after noon to nearby St. John Island, Brother Warner elected to continue dinner at the Moravian Church cantonment, after cannily checking his barometer and noting that the "mercury had fallen only a few lines."

The usual one and a half days' warning of heavy weather would have given Superintendent Cameron and the Royal Mail's captains plenty of time to evaluate conditions, decide on a plan of action, and get under way. Instead, they seem to have gotten not much more than six hours, just enough time to misjudge what was coming.

10

The Desperate Flight of *Rhone* and *Conway*

Capt. Frederick Woolley brought *Rhone* to off St. Peter's Island on October 14. Old salt that he was aside, he still must have been pleased that the westbound crossing from Southampton with 135 passengers on board (3 more than the crew) had been entirely uneventful. In fact, after her maiden voyage, during which tight bearings had caused friction and overheating (a not uncommon problem in new, hand-built steam engines) and a thrilling crossing of the Bay of Biscay, *Rhone*'s career thus far had been something of a triumph.

Woolley came to *Rhone*'s pilothouse directly from command of RMS *Shannon*, on the Brazil mail route. He was an old Royal Mail man with years of experience in command. Woolley had been the master of the pride of the fleet before. Nearly fifteen years earlier he'd commanded the company's first purpose-built iron paddle steamer, RMS *Atrato*, on her maiden voyage across the Atlantic. In 1853, when *Atrato* pulled out of Southampton and headed downriver for Rio the first time, at 3,500 tons and 350 feet, she was thought to be the largest ship afloat.[1] More than simple recognition of his skills as a mariner, command of such a fine ship was—and was meant to be—an honor. Nothing had happened since to dilute the high regard the company's Court of Directors held in their man.

Woolley, a childless widower, had pulled rank on Capt. Robert Woolward and forced the swap of ships and routes with the more junior Woolward that put him in *Rhone* and Woolward back on the route to Rio after less than a year carrying the Caribbean mails. "I was very much put out at this," Woolward confessed in his biography, "but it will be seen that it was ordered for the best, as the *Rhone* was lost on the next voyage. Very few were saved and the captain perished." The exchange put one hundred pounds extra per year into Woolley's pocket and took one hundred pounds from Woolward's, that being the difference in a captain's salary on the two routes. It also left Woolward (1826–1903) to enjoy a long life. In 1892, when Capt. Robert Woolward was promoted to the post of senior captain of the Royal Mail fleet and adorned with the honorific title of "commodore," Woolley and RMS *Rhone* had been dead twenty-five years.[2]

Captain Woolley . . . RMS *Rhone* . . . the West Indies Mail . . . this was the best the Royal Mail Steam Packet Company had, a trifecta. On deck in the presence of passengers, the captain must have presented an imposing and reassuring sight in his blue uniform, with eight of the company's large buttons down both sides of his frock coat and gold lace chevrons topped with more buttons on the cuffs of his sleeves. Three more pairs of buttons on the "skirts," tails, of the coat. A black round hat with a round gold band, the company's flag embroidered above the visor. The very incarnation of the competent British mariner.

Under usual conditions, the anchorage grounds just north of St. Peter's Island, where *Rhone* sailed after bypassing St. Thomas, was accounted a beautiful, peaceful place, "one of the prettiest conceivable" enthused A. W. Nesbitt, an *Illustrated London News* correspondent who wrote a lyrical, contemporary description of this "fairy group of islands":

> On the north is seen Tortola, on the west the Danish island of St. John's, and on the south St. Peter's itself, all picturesque islands covered with most luxuriant tropical foliage, such as bananas, date-trees, cotton-trees, and all kinds of cactus. The water is generally as smooth as a lake, and so clear that one can see the waving of the exquisite sea-fans on the coral reef seven fathoms down, to which the ship is anchored. The coral reef is a steep ridge giving a difference of seven fathoms of water in the length of the ship. . . . The unusual calmness of the water may be

inferred from the fact that on one occasion six of the company's
ships were moored close alongside one another.

For nearly two weeks *Rhone* swung at the hook, while all
around her the practiced routine of preparations for the return
crossing was under way. Under the industrious supervision of
Chief Officer Dalby Topper, junior officers and the crew would
have been too busy to spend much time admiring the setting,
but it's certain that in idle, off-duty hours some grappled for
samples of the colorful coral beneath the hull to take home as
exotic souvenirs or watched fish escape from their predators
below only to be snatched by feeding gulls from above. St.
Peter's Great Harbor is a relatively open anchorage, protected
only by a flat spit of land off to the northeast. The island of
Tortola and its Road Harbor lie several miles off to the north.

We know from the General Regulations that Woolley's
officers should have been minding the barometer all this time,
confirming the daily sinusoidal oscillations that St. Croix's
English language newspaper, the *Avis*, had tracked over the
years: a high at 10:00 a.m., a low at 4:00 p.m., high again
at 10:00 p.m., and low again at 4:00 a.m., this change with
"constant regularity." "If after 4 o'clock," the Regulations
quote *Avis'* correspondent as writing, "either in the morning or
the afternoon, the mercury, instead of rising, continues to fall,
then there is every reason for suspicion."

A sudden, sharp drop in the barometer just before midday
on October 29 alerted Woolley to an approaching storm. Months
later, on January 2, 1868, and perhaps drawing on RMS *Solent's*
log and records, the *Daily Southern Cross*, quoting the *Panama
Star and Herald*, wrote that in the twenty minutes between 11:00
and 11:20 a.m. the barometer at St. Thomas fell an incredible
2.20 inches, from 30.10 to 27.90. If anything like that happened
off St. Peter's Island, Woolley misjudged terribly—fatally—
what was coming. With the barometer at 27.90 inches, the
Star and Herald's possibly imaginative account continued, "it
commenced to blow fearfully from the northwest until 12:30,
when there was a lull for about 15 minutes, during which the
mercury rose to 28.30; at the expiration of the lull the wind

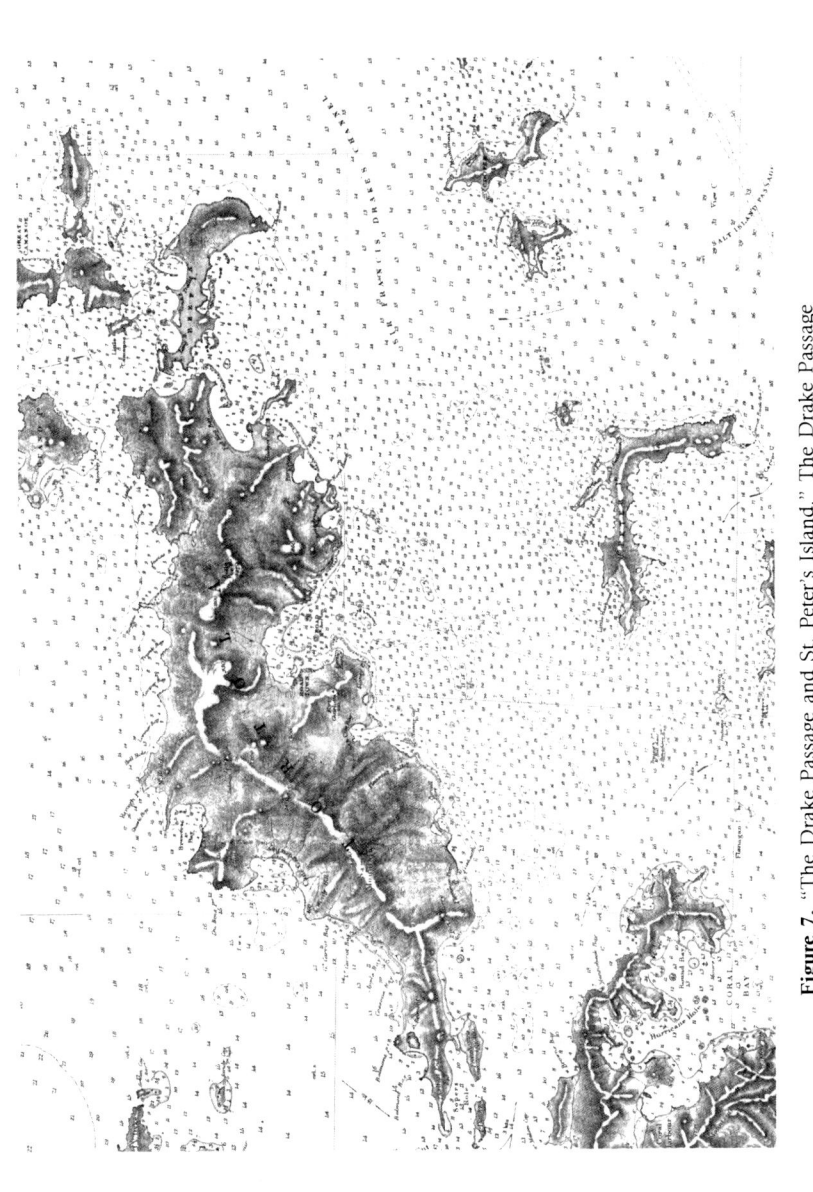

Figure 7. "The Drake Passage and St. Peter's Island." The Drake Passage runs generally east and west between the island of Tortola, to the top (north), and L-shaped St. Peter's Island, to the bottom, in this detail from Admirality chart no. 1993 (1850). *Library of Congress.*

rose with such force from the southeast as to sweep everything before it."

Anchored in five to twelve fathoms of water at Great Harbor, St. Peter's Island, with RMS *Conway* alongside, Woolley was too far from Tortola to be on its lee, protected, side and safely in the wind shadow of the bigger island's 1,500- to 1,700-foot-high spine. As rough water and high winds began to roil the anchorage, both ships got steam up, and soon they were steaming at their anchors, a maneuver designed to ease the tension on the chains that might otherwise unseat the anchors from the bottom and cast the ships adrift.

In Tortola's lee, if her anchor had held, *Rhone* would have been relatively safe from any blow from the north, the "norther" that Woolley feared, although damage to her stack, rigging (the masts, yards, blocks, and lines associated with the sails), small boats stowed topside, and other deck furniture would likely have been significant. Storm winds from any other direction, however, would push the ship irresistibly ashore on the very island that was to have protected her.

Precisely that fate soon seized RMS *Conway* (built in 1846), one of the wooden intercolonial paddle steamers now in the eastern Caribbean for the scheduled rendezvous with *Rhone*. As the storm roared up the Drake Passage, *Conway* steamed away from *Rhone*, fighting her way from Great Harbor toward the imagined safety of Road Harbor, only to be thrown aground on Tortola.

Two other intercolonial paddle steamers, *Solent* (1853, in from Panama the day before) and *Tyne* (1854), both more than twice *Conway*'s size, were just outside the harbor at Charlotte Amalie and had their upper decks wiped clean by the storm, but both survived. Not far away the small paddle steamer *Derwent* (1850), in St. Thomas as the company's reserve ship and standing by to fill in as a replacement for any vessel that fell out of the local schedule, was torn from her mooring in the harbor, heaved up on shore, and destroyed. At about the same time a nine-ton diving bell was picked up by the storm and then dropped near the coal wharves, hundreds of yards away across town.

The iron-hulled screw steamer *Wye* (1853), briefly under the command of Chief Officer Hodgson while her captain was ashore, tried to escape the storm but ended her flight aground and dismasted on little Buck Island, near Tortola. Twenty-eight crew members survived *Wye*'s ensuing breakup and a night in the open on the island, but forty-one did not.

11

Shipwreck on Black Rock

"Hurricanes being whirlwinds," the Barbados governor's memo rightly explained and Captain Woolley knew, "the wind in the circuit of its revolution blows from every point of the compass within the circuit of the whirlwind. The veering of the wind is due to the whirlwind's progress." Today we call hurricanes "cyclones" rather than "whirlwinds," but the meaning is the same. The name describes the characteristic circular pattern of the storm, a configuration recognized as early as 1838 by one Lt. Col. W. Reid of the Royal Engineers. His careful analysis of ships' logs storm data from the early nineteenth century established the cyclonic ("rotatory" was his word) nature of hurricane winds, as apart from the linear track of the slowly revolving storm.

In the Northern Hemisphere the circulation around a hurricane's low-pressure center, its eye, is counterclockwise. As the storm center approaches from the east, increasingly powerful winds come from the north. Once past the bedlam outside the eye wall, all is deceptively calm within. The sky is often wonderfully clear, although filled with confused gulls and other sea birds seeking shelter from winds in the clouds beyond powerful enough to pluck their feathers. As the storm recedes, winds swing to come from the south.

A steamer caught in a cyclone, *Avis* advised and the company's Regulations quoted, should "endeavour to give the land a proper berth [meaning to stay well away from it], and to keep the vessel clear of the center of the storm. For the latter purpose, two things are requisite to be known: viz.; the *direction in which the storm is travelling*, and the *bearing of its center*." As the San Narciso hurricane furiously approached landfall in the Virgin Islands, practically bore-sighted on his ship, Woolley knew neither.

It is possible that St. Thomas' older residents had some premonition of the violence that was about to engulf them as the outer edges of the storm advancing from the east lapped against their island in waves that soon would stand twice as tall as a man. Four memorable hurricanes had hit the island in the last fifty years, beginning with a powerful one in 1819 and including two in the 1820s. Charlotte Amalie's natives in their forties, fifties, and sixties would have had clear memories of the fourth and worst storm, the killer hurricane of August 2, 1837.

HM Packet *Spey*, carrying the royal mail from St. Kitts to St. Thomas via Tortola, sailed into Charlotte Amalie midafternoon on August 6, 1837, having dodged bad weather for days along her route. *Spey* entered St. Thomas, wrote her captain, Lt. R. B. James, RN, to discover that

> There the hurricane of the 2nd appeared to have concentrated all its power, force and fury; for the harbor and town were a scene that baffles all description. Thirty six ships and vessels totally wrecked all around the harbour, among which about a dozen had sunk or capsized at their anchors; some rode it out by cutting away the masts, and upwards of 100 seamen drowned. . . . The harbour is so choked up with wreck and sunken vessels that it is difficult to pick out a berth for a ship to anchor. . . . The fort at the entrance to the harbour is leveled with the foundation, and the 24-pounders thrown down; it looks as if it had been battered to pieces with cannon shot.

If any old-timer connected thirty-year-old memories of the last great storm to premonitions about a coming one, his warning seems to have been ignored. For Woolley's part, he appears to have been unresponsive to the developing weather, probably because he misread it as an Atlantic winter storm from which, he thought, *Rhone* was sheltered. Possibly he was concentrating instead on pushing Superintendent Cameron and Chief Officer Topper hard to get his ship ready for sea, fixed on sailing for Southampton precisely on schedule in a few days time.[1] Whatever the cause, Woolley failed to react in time to the indication of "the evil" to come that had so concerned the Court of Directors, and by the time he did respond, it was too late.

What Woolley might have been thinking late in the morning of October 29, during the last few hours of his life, comes down to us second hand from Captain Hammock of RMS *Conway* through one Capt. Charles Vesey, RN, commanding officer of the 24-gun screw frigate HMS *Doris*, then assigned to the North America and West Indies station. According to Vesey's report to the Admiralty,

> Before leaving Tortola—I boarded the RMS Packet "Conway" and her commander [Hammock] informed me that at 9 am on the 29th he was lashed alongside the "Rhone" off Peter Island— transferring Cargo—that he saw the "Rhone's" Barometer standing at 30 inches, that shortly after—the Commander of the "Rhone" (Captain Woolley) said to him that he did not like the look of the weather, and as the hurricane season was over, it must be a Norther brewing and that he should shift to an anchorage under the Northern Islands—the "Conway" then Cast off—and whilst steaming across was struck by the blast,— the sea rose suddenly, and burst in her ports—the ship being in danger of foundering, . . . The "Rhone's" steam was up just as the "Conway" left her, but Captain Woolley hailed that he could not steer against such a breeze—Shortly after—the "Rhone" began to drag—and then slipped her cables and endeavoured to get to sea, but when the drift and rain cleared off—she was seen on Salt Island.

As the barometer fell and wind and seas rose, caught now in what he erroneously had believed to be a norther and fearful of being blown ashore on the beach at Great Harbor, Woolley abandoned *Rhone*'s anchor ("slipped her cables")—it lies there still—and headed east on a first leg toward open water.

His hastily planned escape route required him to steam across the top of St. Peter's Island, to thread his way seaward through the narrow, deepwater passage past Blonde Reef (its top rising to within just six feet of the surface) and Dead Chest Rock, and then between St. Peter's to starboard and Salt Island to port. Under usual conditions, meaning clear weather and balmy breezes with lookouts posted forward on the bow frequently casting the lead to ensure safe depth of water, this would have been a routine but still pretty bit of seamanship. In heavy weather it would turn out to be impossible, and Woolley's escape attempt quickly turned into disaster.

A survivor, George Holdeman (on *Rhone*'s crew list as captain of the hold but identified as her boatswain in the Leeds, England, *Mercury* issue of November 23), described his ship's last hours to the newspaper's readers, a description that sounds as if *Rhone* passed through the eyewall of the hurricane on her way to destruction:

> We were in a N.W. gale, blowing fresh, when we parted our cable with 60 fathoms in the hawse, and steamed away to sea. After steaming for perhaps an hour it became clear, and in about fifteen minutes we found ourselves close to the shore. The captain then gave orders to turn astern, which we did, and cleared the point. We proceeded steaming through the Gut, and met a south-east wind blowing fearfully heavy; it then became very thick indeed, so that we could scarcely see anything in ship's length. We had been steaming about two hours when I reported to the captain that there was land very close, indeed nearly abreast of us midships on the Port hand: with that the ship went ashore immediately. The captain said to me, "Good Lord, is it even possible?" and I replied, "Yes, sir, the ship's ashore." The captain never spoke to me again, and shortly after a sea struck him in the side and washed him to the top of a skylight. The next sea took him between the ship and the rocks, and I saw no more of him.

Woolley's body was never found, despite Cameron's offer of a reward for it. Most accounts say that none of the *Rhone*'s officers survived the storm, although Vesey allows that the fourth officer, Charles Mathews, managed to cling to some floating bit together with some other members of the crew.

Chief Officer Topper apparently died instantly when he was hit in the head by a yard falling from aloft. According to Holdeman, that had happened an hour or so before Captain Woolley went overboard. Topper's body was found washed ashore on Salt Island the next day, and he was buried there together with the other members of the crew whose bodies had floated in on the surf.

In common with any other form of asphyxiation, drowning does not take long. In very cold water in rare instances, the human body is shocked into a state of something like suspended animation and its slowed metabolism can survive oxygen deprivation for a remarkably long period of time. Young people seem to be especially durable in these infrequent calamities. Nothing like this, however, happens in warm water. The first splash down the airway slams the larynx shut reflexively, but a minute or two later as the body is starved of oxygen, an even more powerful process opens it. Now salt water floods the trachea, filling the lungs with water and foam and creating a massive pulmonary edema, a great puddle in the lungs. The desperate thrashing of arms and legs stops, and unless wave or current action prevents it, the now dead body slowly begins to sink head-down toward the bottom, where it will rest until, days later, putrefying gases lift it back to the surface horribly transformed. The men on deck and their crewmates in *Rhone*'s boiler room died just minutes apart.

Working in the poorly ventilated engine spaces below decks in *Rhone* with fires lit under both boilers would have been difficult and hot normally. The enervating hard labor of moving coal from bunkers to boiler, keeping the fires fed, and raking and removing ash from the grates merited the daily bottle of rehydrating beer and the small per diem payment the company granted for each day steam was up. (Similar special allowances were paid for the other nasty work: loading coal, something that the company usually wanted done by hired common laborers, and cleaning mineral-encrusted boiler flues.)

In ordinary rough weather, with the ship plunging and rolling thorough high seas unpredictably, and forcing unsure footing in congested spaces, the work of firemen and coal trimmers would have been both exhausting and hazardous. Under category 3 hurricane conditions, that same work would have been hellish. As *Rhone* rounded the northeast corner of St. Peter's and, moving under twenty pounds of steam pressure, swung her head to the south, the engineering spaces below decks must have seemed like a deathtrap. No one below could have doubted that the ship was in dire peril; everyone below had spent time on deck sightseeing when *Rhone* was at anchor and knew that the margin for piloting error was microscopically small.

Those crewmembers who did not die on deck or wash over the side to drown lost their lives below when *Rhone* ran up on Black Rock, her keel snapped in half, and her boiler blew up. The cloud of steam instantly formed as cold salt water hit the hot machinery would have scalded the doomed men, likely killing them even before they had time to drown.

Few Victorians could swim, but even a strong swimmer could not have kept himself afloat unassisted under these conditions. If some crewman thought of it early enough, before the storm overwhelmed clear thinking, it is possible that each passenger was issued a cork lifesaving jacket. With *Rhone* in extremis, distribution of the life jackets went well beyond a prudent precaution. The visible presence of these unfamiliar devices would have brought home to the last optimist on board how desperate their situation had become.

Soon after the captain went into the water, Holdeman was also washed off deck. He and five others managed to save themselves by clinging to a bin holding crew hammocks that floated by. If his account is correct, approaching midnight he stepped onto Beef Island—across the width of the Drake Channel from the wreck—wearing nothing but underwear. All his other clothes had been stripped off by the sea.

It's possible that fifteen passengers died in the wreck, perhaps in *Rhone*'s saloon, where they might have been herded together by the crew for safety. Earlier, some passengers had been transferred from little *Conway* while the two were nested alongside, both captains thinking that the larger ship would be the safer one. To be confined in *Rhone*'s saloon as part of a frantically fearful crowd during the ship's last minutes intact and afloat must have been terrifying. Once *Rhone* got under way, everyone inside the small space would have been thrown violently from bulkhead to bulkhead across the deck in a jumble of flailing bodies and heavy furniture with every onrushing wave. This in the dark, with the roar of the storm filling the space. Death must have seemed very close. It was.

Figure 8. "Wreck of the Royal Mail Company's Steam-ship *Rhone* off St. Peter's Island, West Indies." *From the* Illustrated London News, *December 14, 1867.*

Passengers drowned included Mr. and Mrs. Gibbon, Dr. and Mrs. King, and Messrs. Walrond and Yates. Six other men were listed by name, with the notation in *Rhone*'s contemporary records at the National Archives in Kew that "it is believed the following passengers had embarked in the Rhone but it is not altogether certain. If they had embarked they were drowned." These included Messrs. Phillips, Carter, Smith, Farrin, Scott, and Crisp. Nothing else is known about them. Even less is recorded about several others: "Three naval invalids names unknown" might also have been on board *Rhone* and drowned anonymously at the same time. Evidently only one of *Rhone*'s passengers survived. Unofficial descriptions of the tragedy identified him only as an "Italian from Pennsylvania."

Four of the twenty-two crewmen who lived through the wreck of *Rhone* did so by clinging to her foretopsail yard after she sank, hanging in the rigging just clear of the waves but exposed fully to the wind and weather as the storm abated. Some few survivors might have been lucky enough to be washed ashore alive, barely alive. Clambering onto dry land, the sharp volcanic rocks would have shredded their hands and feet as they crawled exhausted from the water.

Still others were carried out of the surf to safety by Salt Island's natives, black freemen who made a meager living on the island by collecting salt from its ponds and selling some of the one thousand pounds or so that was their annual harvest of the mineral. These survivors would have drowned without this succor. The story is that in recognition of their heroism during the hurricane, the rescuers were granted title to plots on the island in exchange for an annual symbolic payment of five pounds of salt to Queen Victoria's royal kitchen.

Once beyond Puerto Rico, San Narciso fell back to tropical storm strength while it chewed along the southern coast of Hispaniola heading for Jamaica, before dropping from available weather records on the morning of October 31 somewhere southeast of Cuba.

12

The Islands after the Hurricane

Malcolm Davis, an Australian from Queensland riding RMS *La Plata* to Jamaica on his first leg home from the United Kingdom, looked around storm-wracked Charlotte Amalie in mid-November—coincidently the day before a tsunami struck the place—and described what he saw:

> The dilapidated remains of the numerous coal wharves, the ruins of the large sheds, tramways, engine-house, and premises, the property of the Royal M.S.P. Company, told too forcibly the tale of the awful tempest that had passed over the island. Looking across the harbor to the east, masts and spars stood out of the quiet water like stubble in a field. . . . The shores of the harbor were girt with a wall several feet high, in places composed of an indescribable and tangled medley of spars, cordage, cargo, flour, fish, cigars, soft goods and bedding. Right and left, crafts from the smallest dingy to the full-masted ship, from the little steam tender of 10 tons to the huge steam packet of 1500, lay high and dry, or stranded on the reefs. . . . At the eastern extremity of the ill-fated floating dock of St. Thomas . . . lie piled, literally one on top of the other, three vessels of an aggregate tonnage of not less than 5000 tons.

The Royal Mail's Court of Directors received the terrible news of the hurricane by telegraph from Superintendent Cameron some days later. "Fearful hurricane at St. Thomas on October 29," Cameron reported, continuing manfully through the dreadful muster report to a brave conclusion: "The Rhone steamer lost at Peter Island; the Wye steamer lost at Buck

Figure 9. "St. Thomas Harbour after the Storm, October 31, 1867." *From the Illustrated London News, November 30, 1867.*

Island. The Conway ashore on Tortola, the Derwent ashore on St. Thomas. The Tyne and Solent steamers dismasted but serviceable. Fifty ships on shore. Terrible loss of life. Town in ruins. Fever over. The company's service will be maintained. The Douro will leave homewards November 4."

Not surprisingly, in the United Kingdom the news immediately prompted "a sustained and serious fall" in the value of shares of the RMSP Company. According to the Belfast, Ireland, *News-Letter*, down to half their value of eighteen months earlier.

It fell to Capt. Ebenezer Kemp of *Douro* to deliver the eyewitness details to Southampton in person when he arrived in England mid-November. (*Douro*'s survival would develop to be less a pardon than a stay of execution. She sank off Finisterre out of Lisbon bound for Southampton in April 1882 following a collision, holed by the Spanish steamer *Yrurac Bat* en route to Liverpool. *Douro*'s captain and fourteen other members of the crew died, as did six of her sixty passengers. Her memorial monument in Southampton's Old Cemetery is not far from *Rhone*'s. It celebrates the sacrifice of the lost ship's company, who died saving most of their passengers.)

The *Rhone* tragedy hit families in Southampton, the transatlantic fleet's homeport, especially hard. Husbands, fathers, and sons gone forever. Southampton's mayor and his big city counterpart, the lord mayor of London, quickly joined in establishing a relief fund for seafaring English families suddenly facing destitution and for the 1,056 in the distant colony now homeless. The appeal for charity reached the royal palace and touched Queen Victoria, who contributed two hundred pounds.

Charity did not come so easily for some. Arthur Rumbold, writing from Tortola to Governor Hill of Antigua on November 12, first reported the devastation of Road Town (half the houses destroyed, one-quarter severely damaged, and all the rest partially so), and on Virgin Gorda, and Jost van Dyke. He then continued:

I feel most profoundly the misery of so many individuals and

families, but I am sure that your Excellency will recognize the
utter impossibility of immediately applying a remedy, I have no
desire to avert the exercise of a just or generous sympathy, but
everyone acquainted with the West Indies must know what gross
fabrications the negro will make when he entertains the hope of
gaining bread without exertion: Many who are not losers by the
Hurricane and who were content to eke out existence in a hovel
rather than to labor for an honest livelihood, rush forward now
with a specious tale of woe and succeed in imposing on those
who are unacquainted with their true position and the real extent
of their loss.

Rumbold was clearly proud to report to his superior that
he had relocated paupers from the destroyed "Poor-house" into
the cells of the "gaol" (jail), leaving the cell doors open for
ventilation. Prisoners and their "Turnkey" (guard) first being
moved to a "fire-proof store."

A later report from Road Town, in January 1868 to "Her
Majesty's Secretary of State, the Duke of Buckingham and
Chandos," provided an accounting of the lord mayor's fund's
disbursements in the British West Indies.[1] A number of country
districts and assorted small islands received £6,033. Road
Town, where twenty-two had died, got the next most, £1,510;
Virgin Gorda got £455; Jost Van Dyck, £216; St. Peter's Island
(*Rhone*'s temporary refuge), £166; and the West End, £160.

If the story of the land grant is apocryphal, then Salt
Island's brave residents didn't get much for their courage or
to compensate them for their own losses from the storm that
erased their homes from the island and flooded their salt pans
with unwelcome fresh water. They received only £70 in relief
assistance from the metropolis, the least of any beneficiary of
the relief fund.

The lord mayor's fund provided aid only to the denizens of
the British Virgin Islands. Hurricane survivors living on Sankt
Croix, Sankt Thomas, and Sankt Jan had to look to Copenhagen
for assistance.

In an era long before oceanic weather forecasting, before
building codes, emergency management agencies, and timely

evacuation, San Narciso hit entirely without warning, and its destruction ashore and in adjacent waters was terrible. An early census of ship losses from the storm reported some forty-six vessels flying the flags of seven nations sunk or run aground and destroyed. The lost included five steamers and forty-one sailing ships, among them boats as inconsequential as the modestly named Danish tugs *Urchin* and *Pigmy* and ships as imposing as *Great Britain* and *Colombian*. A more accurate later count would be even greater, fifty-eight of sixty ships in the harbor were sunk by the storm. All the steamers lost but one would be from the RSMP's fleet, a loss to the company the *New York Times* estimated at the then-huge sum of $12 million.

The first word of the calamity came to New York during early November, in news reports from Puerto Rico relayed through Havana. (At the time the Cuban capital was suffering its own catastrophe, an epidemic of cholera, "confined," the unnamed reporter elaborated sounding almost pleased, "almost entirely to negroes, Chinese, and the lower classes.")

It took time for anything like an accurate account of the calamity to reach the outside world. An example, the island of Tortola, the *New York Times* first reported hysterically, had been entirely submerged under storm waters for eight hours; 10,000—a guess as to the number of inhabitants—were said to have drowned. "We are assured," the *Times* intoned morbidly on November 15, quoting the *Puerto Rico Bulletin*, "that the island of Tortola has disappeared beneath the sea." In that Tortola's "usual elevation" rises to more than one-quarter mile above sea level, the fantastic early coverage did little more than expose the *Times*' topographic ignorance and the feverish imagination of the paper's source.

Four days later Tortola's fate was less certain, and the *Times* was moved to confess that "that there are only rumors of serious disaster . . . but no definite facts, and the reports are evidently greatly exaggerated." Good news followed on November 23, more than three weeks after the storm. "Tortola," the paper advised reassuringly, "suffered severely from the recent hurricane, but remains at its usual elevation above the surface of the sea."

"Heavy loss of life and great destruction of property" was said to have visited Santo Domingo. Likewise, the losses on southern Puerto Rico were "incalculable," with hundreds dead, thousands homeless, immense numbers of cattle killed, the cane crop destroyed, and fields swept bare. Nothing had been heard from the more remote, central part of the island. The best modern estimate of lives lost in San Narciso is found in a National Oceanic and Atmospheric Administration technical memorandum dated May 1995: an oddly imprecise "greater than 811."

Even as hurricane wreckage still sloshed on the tide, the Caribbean's terrible year of 1867 wrenched the dazed and depopulated islands one last time. Early in the morning of November 18, three weeks after San Narciso had stormed through the archipelago, a powerful submarine earthquake roiled the Anegada Passage between Anguilla and Virgin Gorda. The epicenter seems to have been near Virgin Gorda, just east of Tortola, and lay perhaps only twenty miles below the surface. Two sharp shocks, separated by ten minutes or so, signaled an abrupt rise (now believed to have been about thirty feet) in the depth of the seafloor along ten or twenty miles of submarine fault. The earthquake, estimated at 7.5 surface magnitude, promptly produced two tsunamis that propagated quickly throughout the eastern Caribbean, two powerful pulses of seismic energy almost concealed under a seemingly innocent surface ripple in the water until they approached the shallows.

Naturally the islands closest to the passage were hit first, although not necessarily the hardest. The height of the wave running onshore depended on the slope facing the origin, among other things. The usual pattern was repeated here, an initial recession of water that astonished naïve observers, the ocean first withdrawing mysteriously seaward and exposing a part of the never seen harbor bottom, followed by a powerful onrushing wall as the water raced back in devastating strength. In less than one hour, the wave front washed against the Grenadines, southernmost of the Windward Islands, and moments later it hit the South American coast.

Although some contemporary accounts spoke fearfully about sixty-foot waves advancing up the beach (as big as a six-story building and more than two times larger than the Indian Ocean killer of December 2004, which it resembled in many ways), and one only slightly less breathless eyewitness report spoke of a forty-foot wave at Water Island, modern computer modeling suggests that the tallest tsunamis were probably those which flooded Deshaies and Sainte-Rose, Guadeloupe, perhaps thirty feet in amplitude, thirty feet trough to crest. (It was here at Sainte-Rose that eyewitness reports had said the wave stood sixty feet.) St. Croix and St. Thomas were likely hit by waves between twenty and twenty-five feet high.

The tsunami at Charlotte Amalie battered the waterfront yet again, barely three weeks after the hurricane had shredded ships in the anchorage. RMS *La Plata*, coaling at anchor three miles outside the inner harbor, near Water Island, was fortunate to survive. *La Plata*, 2,400 tons and built for Cunard but bought off the ways in 1851 by the RMSP, had arrived at St. Thomas early on Sunday, November 17, after a fifteen-day crossing from Southampton. While coaling the next afternoon she was caught by the great wave. A contemporary watercolor sketch showing RMS *La Plata* with a coal lighter alongside, stern-to the maw of the breaking tsunami, by Capt. J. Sumpter Mitchell of the RMSP, was the basis of a woodcut illustration of the moment that appeared the *Illustrated London News* weeks later.

Malcolm Davis, now safely at home, described to readers of the January 7, 1868, *Brisbane Courier* the approach of the huge wave. Captain Revett and *La Plata*'s other officers on board, he wrote sounding as if he were embarked,

> by their look gave no hope; the passengers silently and calmly awaited their inevitable doom. But God in His mercy spared them: a wall of water broke with a most deafening roar on the spur of Water Island and sensibly lessened the impetus of the wave. The eddy, which had proved so fatal to small craft, under the providence of God, was the safety of the La Plata. It canted her round, so that her stern met the sea which, as it thundered down on her washed the dingy out of the stern davits, smashed the starboard lifeboat to match wood, twisted the davits like pin wire, and stove in the bulwarks, flooding the cabins and lower

Figure 10. "The Earthquake Wave at St. Thomas Striking the Royal Mail Steam-ship *La Plata.*" *From the* Illustrated London News, *November 28, 1867.*

deck: but the ship was saved—buoyant as she was, she rose to the wave, up and down she went . . . and then she floated again in as quiet a sea as ever.

USS *Susquehanna*, flagship of the North Atlantic Squadron, and her escort, USS *De Soto*, were also in St. Thomas. *De Soto* was shoved into the port's iron dry dock, holed in several places, and kept afloat only by furious pumping. *Susquehanna* was more fortunate. The damage his flagship sustained, the squadron commander reported to Secretary of the Navy Gideon Welles, was "not material."

The wave then sped south across the thirty miles between St. Thomas and St. Croix and hit Frederiksted, on St. Croix's west coast, where it lifted and tossed ashore the auxiliary screw sloop USS *Monongahela*, in port also supporting the American diplomatic team then negotiating with the Danes to buy St. Thomas and St. John.

Some idea of the power of the tsunami comes from the mass of the ship suddenly lofted onto dry land. *Monongahela* was 227 feet long, 38 feet in beam, and drew 17 feet of water. She displaced 2,078 tons and carried a crew of 176. All that flipped ashore in an instant . . . four men killed and one terribly injured. *Monongahela* remained near Frederiksted like a beached whale for six months before finally being successfully refloated in May 1868 and towed to New York. Her repairs took years to effect. It was many years, too, before the United States again considered purchase of the islands.

Once more small boats everywhere were sunk, and beachfront structures (those few standing still or rebuilt since San Narciso) were destroyed. Loss of life was mercifully relatively light, probably because few of the survivors of yellow fever and San Narciso had moved back near the water so soon.

The Virgins lie not far south of the 560-mile-long Puerto Rico trench, the great gash in the crust of the earth that underlies the Atlantic's deepest waters. The North American and Caribbean tectonic plates bound the trench to the north and the south, respectively. The region is geologically active. Earthquakes and tsunamis are not uncommon here—twelve major and many minor waves have washed the Caribbean islands since 1530—and more are certain to occur.

On November 24 the *New York Times* printed a roster of ships lost during Hurricane St. Narciso. The information came, again, from the Virgin Islands via Havana and passed through many hands on its way to Manhattan, so it is certain there were errors in the information about ships lost and damaged. Much better than rumor, but not exactly fact. The *Times*' report revealed that forty-one ships had sunk in the storm; the wreck of one was condemned and sold for one dollar. Another thirty-four had run or been put aground and were "seriously injured."

Drawing on unidentified sources, on November 27 the *Panama Star and Herald* published its own inventory of the vessels "foundered, driven ashore, or otherwise injured" by the hurricane. That paper's mournful tally of eighteen steamers and sixty-three sailing vessels included among the latter a representative assortment of brigs, barques, brigantines, schooners, and sloops, every rig one could expect to see in Caribbean trade. Twenty-eight ships listed by name, six of them belonging to the RMSP Company, were of British registry. Six American vessels were in the total: *Sarah Newman*, "in the mud"; *Charles Sprague*, a "total wreck"; *Aberdeen*, dismasted with eight feet of water in her hold; *Nelly Gay* and *Mesota*, both washed aground; and *Clinton*, sunk. Vessels registered in France, Spain, Denmark, Holland, Norway, and Venezuela made up the balance.

In 1868 the Royal Mail would be chased from the St. Thomas terminal by rampant yellow fever. The tiny female *Aedes* mosquito and the hemorrhagic fever it inflicted got the credit for the move, but the fact that access to the harbor was still blocked by the sunken hulk of *Colombian* and that the company's facilities ashore had been completely destroyed and would have to be entirely rebuilt probably forced the relocation decision. Whatever the true cause, the RMSP's terminal port for transatlantic steamers was shifted in 1868 from St. Thomas across the full length of the Gulf of Mexico to Colón, on the Isthmus of Panama. After 1868 company ships still stopped at Charlotte Amalie on local service, but vindicating Trollope, the port was no longer the hub of the hemisphere.

13

Jeremiah Murphy's Salvage Operations

Thirty-six years after the Congress of Vienna reshaped Europe following the Napoleonic Wars, but only three after the Continent was roiled by revolutions from one end to the other, London hosted the Great Exhibition of 1851. Set in Hyde Park inside the spectacular Crystal Palace—a remarkable structure enclosing 770,000 square feet and made of nearly 294,000 individual panes of glass supported in a unique cast-iron building frame assembled in modules—the event was a perfect opportunity for Victorians to boast of their imperial success and a seemingly insurmountable lead in global industrialization, and to somewhat smugly point to the undisturbed political tranquility in the home islands as general evidence of British moral as well as scientific and technological superiority.

Among the featured thirteen thousand exhibits in the Crystal Palace was Stand No. 426, a display on open water diving. With some justification, this was yet another area in which the British claimed world leadership. Thanks to the work of two countrymen, the Deane brothers and one Augustus Siebe (granted an Austrian, but an expatriate living and working as an engineer in London for many years), the technology of diving had made enormous strides since the 1820s, when Charles Deane first thought of converting his proprietary design for a fireman's smoke mask into a diving helmet.

The Deane display of diving apparatus at the Great Exhibition was a great crowd pleaser: a large glass tank—imagine a huge aquarium incongruously topped with patriotic flags and the three ostrich feathers of the Prince of Wales' emblem, and flanked by statues of dolphins—contained a water-filled diorama of miniature divers on the seafloor below a support boat on the surface. Off to one side of the tank, a full-sized suit ("diving dress") and a three-cylinder air pump completed the Deanes' impressive stand.

John Deane's success to date was attested to by the *Illustrated Exhibitor*. Equipped with this apparatus, the exposition's newsletter reported somewhat breathlessly that, "man may leave his native element and enter another, fatal to him under ordinary circumstances, and wade among the unknown parts of the deep with ease, confidence, and perfect safety, carrying forward any work it may be desired to execute."

Before the 1800s diving was more a matter of physiology than technology. "Free diving," diving simply holding one's breath, let its adepts (Japanese pearl and Greek sponge divers, for example) get down to ninety feet or so and remain submerged for as long as two minutes. Free diving's obvious limitations led to very early experiments with air-delivery systems in which ingenuity, limited only by available materials and muscle power, quickly ran up against the unknown limits of the human body under water. Even so, in the fifteenth and sixteenth centuries, divers in very rudimentary gear equipped with specialized tools probably managed to salvage sunken ships' weapons and cargoes, although for the most part contemporary illustrations of their diving dress show rigs that almost certainly would not have worked. Nor, for that matter, would da Vinci's designs of the early sixteenth century have worked.

By 1850 John Deane had been down to 132 feet and remained below (although not so deep) for as much as six hours in one dive. His wreck dives would include recovery operations on ships sunk during the Crimean War in the Black Sea.

The wreckage of the merchant fleet and harbor equipment destroyed in the tight roadsteads of the Virgin Islands congested them beyond use, nearly beyond imagination. The bottom would have been covered with holed hulls, the sea's surface with all manner of flotsam, floating ship timbers and planks, and miscellaneous gear mingling promiscuously with bits and pieces of shoreside houses and shops blown apart by the wind.

The islands of the Caribbean were firmly tied into the Atlantic trading system and not able to sustain themselves as they had been in the simple days prior to discovery by Columbus; thus clearing their waters and harbors was an essential part not only of immediate disaster relief but also of longer term economic recovery. Fortunately the technology of wreck diving was sufficiently advanced approaching the 1870s to make such an enormous effort feasible. Fortunately, too, an expert diver, Jeremiah Murphy, lived not far away on Grand Turk Island.

Among others, Murphy and his two brothers from Ireland, Andrew and Denis, were hired by the Danish government to clear wrecks in Charlotte Amalie Harbor after the hurricane. All of their equipment, the essential engines, pumps, and diving dress, came from the United Kingdom. The effort took Murphy five years, from 1868 to 1872, and cost him both brothers, who died in separate accidents during the operation.

The record suggests that Murphy spent only one day diving on *Rhone*, six hours altogether in two dives separated by a half-hour break at the surface. Modern dive tables would not permit so much time at depth with so little time on the surface, but the physiological risks of entrapped nitrogen from extended breathing of compressed air were not understood then, and despite the sobering loss of his brothers, Murphy evidently still believed his practices were safe. He must have known the location of *Rhone*'s bullion room and of its single padlocked door opening only onto the orlop deck, because in those few hours Murphy managed to bring up £60,000 worth of gold bullion and coin . . . and drinks for dinner. Perhaps he came up with other valuable bits and pieces, too—the safes in the captain's and purser's cabins possibly would have contained attractive salvage—and with her keel broken recovery of the ship would have been impossible.

Murphy wasn't the only salvor drawn to St. Croix. The harbor's troublesome floating iron dry dock, built from a design by Sir Frederick Bramwell (1818–1903), was finally successfully raised in January 1871 after George Blaxland, an English engineer and the son of a shipyard chief, designed and built the locks through which compressed air was blown into the dock's pontoons to expel water.

It's not clear who, Murphy or Blaxland, played the key role in lifting the steamer *Colombian* from the bottom where she had lain closing the channel to the Charlotte Amalie harbor. The unlucky vessel had barely arrived in port when the storm hit; she finally left under her own power in March 1872. Different accounts credit one or the other man with this achievement, but the citizens of St. Thomas presented Murphy with a certificate and medal for the achievement, so the greater part of the credit was probably his, although the technology of using compressed air for lifting wrecks was a Blaxland specialty.

14

Rhone Today

In 1976, on a roll from the intoxicating success of his two-year-old novel *Jaws*, author Peter Benchley turned out another saltwater thriller, *The Deep*. The two films were very different stories and when released met very different public receptions. Directed by Steven Spielberg, *Jaws* was a brilliant popular success. So much so that Benchley will be fortunate if the word doesn't turn up on his tombstone. It will certainly be the highlight of his obituary. Director Peter Yates' *The Deep*, on the other hand, never achieved mega-hit status. Its more measured reception unfairly raised the possibility at least that Benchley, a former journalist and presidential speechwriter, was a one-trick pony.

Jaws starred the perfect predator, *Carcharodon carcharias*, a huge great white shark that snapped up swimmers off Amity, Long Island, as if they were warm hors d'oeuvres on a buffet table. The mouthy shark, one of several cranky hydro-mechanical robots in real life (1975, when the movie was shot, was too early for the computerized special effects that would dazzle movie goers just a few years later), was a heart-stopping fright on film. Coupled with composer John Williams' two-note string orchestra theme that seemingly echoed the shark's metabolism, or appetite, Benchley's imaginary great white probably kept wary swimmers out of the ocean for several summers. So powerful was the fearsome imagery that thirty years later a television network could still squeeze some mileage out of Benchley's hoary idea. This last time around CBS substituted bikini-clad coeds on spring break from college instead of the good citizens of Amity for chum.

Although Columbia's copycat publicity poster for Benchley's new movie deliberately hinted at the underwater menace that made *Jaws* so successful, *The Deep* turned out to be not nearly as mesmerizing as *Jaws*. Jacqueline Bisset in a wet white T-shirt was captivating enough, as toothsome in her way as was the shark in its, but the plot—honeymooning tourists diving for adventure entangled with criminals diving for drugs—lacked the visceral punch of the first movie.

Too bad. The underappreciated real star of *The Deep* was RMS *Rhone*, with her wreck off Salt Island standing in for the fictitious SS *Goliath*. *Goliath*, the plot had it, sank off Bermuda during World War II with a load of morphine ampoules on board.

Peter Yates' movie is a good way for landlubbers to see what remains of the *Rhone* after more than a century on the bottom. *Rhone*'s wreck lies in several large pieces in twenty-five to eighty feet of water off Salt Island's Black Rock Point. Her stern and bow form a large right angle, the sharp break in the hull suggesting the violence of the breakup. *Rhone*'s stern is oriented generally east–west with the rudder and screw closest to shore. The tips of the ship's great bronze screw blades are clearly shorn off, ground flat on the rock as the ship ran aground with the prop spinning. Another indication of the forces at work when *Rhone* sank. Her prop shaft and engine gear box are clearly identifiable in the wreckage field, as are the remains of the boiler. Near or in between these two large structures are other bits of wreckage recognizable under encrusted coral and sponges as her condenser, two masts, boat davits, and some ship's anchor chain.

Today RMS *Rhone* is the centerpiece of the British Virgin Islands' Wreck of the Rhone Marine Park, a 798-acre reservation managed by the Virgin Islands' National Parks Trust, which also includes Dead Chest Island, an uninhabited outcropping that features a pair of salt ponds and little else. The protecting park is some thirty years old. In between 1867 and 1980, and beginning with the sanctioned salvage operations immediately after the ship went down, *Rhone* was easily accessible and highly vulnerable to marine souvenir hunters.

Not surprisingly all the "good bits," the kind of trophy relics such as engine instruments, porthole covers, and dishware that divers and looters are drawn to, have been removed from the wreck long since. Some few of these are exhibited at the Saba Rock Nautical Museum and Gift Shop, the others likely rest uncatalogued in private collections worldwide.

Figure 11. The Loss of RMS *Rhone*, a British Virgin Islands postage stamp, first day of issue, April 16, 1884.

Stamp collections, too, hold reminders of RMS *Rhone*'s last minutes afloat. The famous wreck, even after the weather cleared not quite in sight of Road Town, the British Virgin Islands' capital across the Channel, has been commemorated three times on Virgin Islands postage stamps: in the 1970s, 1980s, and again in the 1990s, each time slightly differently. The second of the three was issued in 1884 to mark the 250th anniversary of *Lloyd's List*, the shipping newsletter.

The stamp designs are all riffs in miniature on William Frederick Mitchell's watercolor painting of *Rhone* atop Black Rock, a homage to the artist as well as to the ship. Mitchell, deaf since an attack of scarlet fever in childhood took away his hearing, did some 3,500 paintings of ships at sea either on private commission or as illustrations for books, each carefully numbered by the artist. The wreck of the *Rhone*, number 203, came early in his large body of work. Mitchell's illustrations included many in the superb two-volume *The Royal Navy in a Series of Illustrations* (1872) and in editions of *Brassey's Naval Annual* after 1886.

Figure 12. The *Rhone* and *Wye* monument in Southampton Old Cemetery in Southampton, England. *Photo courtesy Valerie Ferguson, Friends of Southampton Old Cemetery.*

The summer after the wreck, July 1868, *Rhone* was replaced in the Royal Mail's transatlantic packet schedule by RMS *Neva*, just then finishing construction at the Caird and Company shipyard and scheduled for delivery to an operator in Bremen, Germany. Slightly larger than *Rhone*, *Neva* boasted the same exalted level of accommodation for her 272 first-class passengers, who could take their ease in a saloon richly paneled in oak, adorned by gilded trim, and furnished in handsome walnut. When *Neva* sailed, she was the seventh ship from this popular yard on the Clyde to fly the company's flag.

Most bodies of the *Rhone*'s crew and passengers were never recovered from the sea. Those few that were found were buried ashore on Salt Island. A memorial to the dead, lost, and found stands thousands of miles away, in Southampton Old Cemetery in Southampton, England, near the heart of the old English port city from which *Rhone* had sailed with such confidence on her last cruise. Sadly this handsome monument recalling RMS *Rhone* and her sister ship, *Wye*, was vandalized in October 2011, after this photo was taken. Repairs have not yet been effected and the Friends of Southampton Old Cemetery are still collecting donations for this purpose.

Rhone's bronze bell, which once signaled the half hours and the change of watches on board on the ship, now hangs in the steeple of St. Thomas' Anglican Church on the island of South Caicos. Its tolling is all that's left alive of the *Rhone*.

NOTES

Chapter 1. The Millwall Ironworks and Shipbuilding Company

1. In 1866 SS *Great Eastern*, otherwise unemployed, was char-
    tered to lay an undersea cable between Europe and North
    America. She was the only vessel big enough to carry alone
    the requisite 2,500 miles of cable. The first two attempts in
    1857–58, featuring USS *Niagara* and HMS *Agamemnon*,
    each carrying half, had failed, but this third try was a success,
    finally linking the two continents by telegraph and heralding
    our era of near-instant communication. In the quirky open-
    ing ceremonies of the London 2012 Olympics, actor Kenneth
    Branagh mimed *Great Eastern*'s designer, the brilliant Victo-
    rian engineer Isambard Kingdom Brunel (1806–59).

Chapter 2. The Royal Mail Steam Packet Company

1. The town was named after the long-suffering wife of King
    Christian V of Denmark and Norway. Charlotte Amalie
    (1650–1714) was the mother of eight of his fourteen children,
    the other six being the progeny of her rival, Amelia Moth, the
    king's mistress and his tutor's daughter. Christian V, born in
    1646, ruled from 1670 until his death in a hunting accident in
    1699.
2. The best-known of these early RMSP ships was probably
    RMS *Trent* (the first of three with that name) in the fleet from
    1841 until 1865, and in 1866 at Woolwich the last of the first
    fourteen to be broken up. Near noon on November 8, 1861,
    with Confederate diplomats James Mason and John Slidell
    on board, RMS *Trent*, Capt. James Moir, commanding, out
    of Havana for St. Thomas with the Mexican and Cuban mails
    was stopped on the high seas by USS *San Jacinto*, under the
    command of the mercurial Capt. Charles Wilkes, USN--he of
    the 1838–42 United States Exploring Expedition. The illegal
    removal of the two Southerners provoked a crisis in U.S. rela-
    tions with the UK during the Civil War that was eased only by

a formal apology from Secretary of State Seward in December to his British counterpart and the men's subsequent release.

Chapter 3. Royal Mail Ship *Rhone*

1. In 1855 a railway replaced the mules. This awkward pattern was duplicated in the Eastern Hemisphere. For thirty years, until the Suez Canal was finished in 1869, the short route from Europe to India (meaning not around Cape Horn) included a taxing eighty-four-mile overland leg between Alexandria on the Mediterranean and Port Suez on the Red Sea. That route and the service was the inspiration of Thomas Waghorn (1800–1850), a former Royal Navy lieutenant.
2. Secularized into "Peter Island," the entire island is the site of a privately owned, four-star resort and spa today.

Chapter 4. Riding the *Rhone*

1. Alexis Benoit Soyer (1809–58) established an enviable reputation as chef de cuisine to members of the English peerage soon after he arrived from France in 1831. Soyer, perhaps history's first celebrity chef, was known for good works as well as good food, for the authorship of several cookbooks, and for the invention of a superior camp stove. He ran a charity soup kitchen in Ireland during the terrible famine and a demonstration military mess during the Crimean War. Original Soyer stoves were in use by Australian military units as late as the First World War.
2. This "frozen water trade" had its start in an inspiration by a young Bostonian, one Frederick Tudor, and would continue practically through the century, successfully moving its highly perishable product from New England as far as India, at the outset on ships propelled by sail.

Chapter 5. Safety at Sea

1. The ancients had grappled with the same problems long before Antonio and Shylock. The legal code attributed to Hammurabi, king of ancient Babylon in 1800 BC, almost four millennia before RMS *Rhone*, forgave loans made against lost ships.

Chapter 6. The Royal Mail Steam Packet Company in Operation

1. Not so much by the turn of the century and even less so in the years after 1926, when under the aggressive leadership of then-chairman Owen Philipps, First Baron Kylsant, the RMSP acquired the White Star Line and saw its fleet balloon to 538 ships, surpassing the Cunard and P&O fleets to become the world's largest. The expansion was unwittingly timed to catch the global economic depression. In mid-1931 Philipps (1863–1937) and his auditor were charged with falsifying company accounts and deceiving would-be investors. He was found guilty of one count, convicted, lost his appeal, and spent a year at London's marvelously named Wormwood Scrubs Prison. In August 1932 the company emerged from reorganization, pared down and under new management as the Royal Mail Lines, Ltd.

Chapter 9. "Sudden and Imminent Peril"

1. San Narciso, or Saint Narcissus, in the second century was the thirtieth bishop of Jerusalem. His feast day falls on October 29.

Chapter 10. The Desperate Flight of *Rhone* and *Conway*

1. The National Maritime Museum holds a dramatic 1864 painting by William Mitchell of RMS *Atrato* steaming downwind in foul weather with storm canvas up. She's heeled over sharply to starboard, with practically her entire portside paddle exposed. In the foreground, flotsam in the water suggests a ship has gone down nearby.
2. Woolward's half-century career with the company ended in honored retirement in 1894, the year he published his autobiography, *Nigh on Sixty Years at Sea*, to good reviews. "Very entertaining reading," enthused *The Times*. "Capt. Woolward . . . tells his story with the frankness of an old salt. He has a keen sense of humor, and his stories are endless and entertaining." The epitaph on his tombstone at St. Lawrence Church, Ramsgate, also suggests "Old Woolward" might have had a puckish sense of humor: "This marks the wreck of Robert Woolward who sailed the seas for 55 years. When resurrec-

tion gun fires the wreck will be raised by the Angelic Salvage Company, surveyed, and if found worthy, refitted and sent on the voyage of eternity."

Chapter 11. Shipwreck on Black Rock

1. Cameron (1821–78) was no stranger to disaster at sea. Almost twenty years earlier, on February 12, 1847, he'd been one of sixty-two passengers in RMS *Tweed*, steaming off course at night through a "norther" between Havana and Veracruz when she ran aground on the Alacrán Reef and broke up, drowning seventy-two crew and passengers. Seventy-nine survived, marooned for days on the reef until rescued by the Spanish brig *Emilio*. Later that year he told the story in a book, *The Wreck of the West Indies Steam-ship Tweed by an Eye Witness*. Cameron spent thirty years on St. Thomas as the RMSP's superintendent, during which time he was knighted by the Danish king, styling himself "Sir" thereafter.

Chapter 12. The Islands after the Hurricane

1. Richard Temple-Grenville (1823–99), the third and last duke of Buckingham and Chandos, served briefly and without distinction as secretary of state for the colonies between March 1867 and December 1868. The high point of his career in government was five years as governor of Madras, India, where he might have caught the disease that eventually killed him. Buckingham had the misfortune of being the son and grandson of two extravagant wastrels. The line conveniently ran out of money and male issue at about the same time, not much more than a century after the birth of the first duke in 1776.

SELECTED BIBLIOGRAPHY

Ackroyd, Peter. *The Thames: The Biography*. New York: Nan A. Talese, 2008.

"Agreement for Foreign-Going Ship." Signed September 26, 1865. Board of Trade Records. The National Archives, Kew.

Brooks, Colin, ed. *The Royal Mail Case Rex V. Lord Kyslant and Another*. Edinburgh: Wall, Hodge, 1933.

Bushnell, T. A. *"Royal Mail": A Centenary History of the Royal Mail Line, 1839–1939*. London: Trade and Travel, 1939.

[Cameron, John C.] *The Wreck of the West Indies Steam-ship Tweed by an Eye Witness*. London: Society for the Promotion of Christian Knowledge, 1847.

Goebel, Erik. "Management of the Port of St. Thomas, Danish West Indies, during the Nineteenth and Early Twentieth Centuries." *Northern Mariner/Le Marin du Nord* 7, no. 4 (October 1997): 45–63.

Kenton, Phil J., and Harry G. Parsons. *Early Routings of the Royal Mail Steam Packet Company, 1842–1879*. East Grinstead, UK: Postal Historical Society, 1999.

Nichol, Stuart. *Macqueen's Legacy*. 2 vols. Stroud, UK: Tempus Publishing, 2001.

Reid, Sir William. *An Attempt to Develop the Law of Storms by Means of Facts, Arranged According to Place and Time*. London: J. Weale, 1838.

Rhone Reg. No. 52792, Official Log Book No. 5. Board of Trade Records. The National Archives, Kew.

Trollope, Anthony. *The West Indies and the Spanish Main*. London: Chapman and Hall, 1859.

Woolward, Robert. *Nigh on Sixty Years at Sea*. London: Digby, Long, 1894.

_____. *Royal Mail Steam Packet Company General Regulations 1860*. London: Mitchell and Son, 1860.

About the Author

Andrew C. A. Jampoler lives in the Lost Corner of Loudoun County, Virginia, with his wife, Susan, a professional geographer, and their two golden retrievers. He is an alumnus of Columbia College and the School of International and Public Affairs, both of Columbia University, in New York City, and of the Foreign Service Institute's School of Language Study.

Earlier in life Jampoler spent a year in South Vietnam and commanded a land-based maritime patrol aircraft squadron and a naval air station during twenty-four years on active duty as an aviator in the U.S. Navy. Later he was a senior sales and marketing executive in the international aerospace industry. He has been writing history books and magazine articles for the past dozen years.

He is a certified SCUBA diver and, together with his children and grandchildren, has dived on the wreck of the *Rhone*.

The Naval Institute Press is the book-publishing arm of the U.S. Naval Institute, a private, nonprofit, membership society for sea service professionals and others who share an interest in naval and maritime affairs. Established in 1873 at the U.S. Naval Academy in Annapolis, Maryland, where its offices remain today, the Naval Institute has members worldwide.

Members of the Naval Institute support the education programs of the society and receive the influential monthly magazine *Proceedings* or the colorful bimonthly magazine *Naval History* and discounts on fine nautical prints and on ship and aircraft photos. They also have access to the transcripts of the Institute's Oral History Program and get discounted admission to any of the Institute-sponsored seminars offered around the country.

The Naval Institute's book-publishing program, begun in 1898 with basic guides to naval practices, has broadened its scope to include books of more general interest. Now the Naval Institute Press publishes about seventy titles each year, ranging from how-to books on boating and navigation to battle histories, biographies, ship and aircraft guides, and novels. Institute members receive significant discounts on the Press's more than eight hundred books in print.

Full-time students are eligible for special half-price membership rates. Life memberships are also available.

For a free catalog describing Naval Institute Press books currently available, and for further information about joining the U.S. Naval Institute, please write to:

Member Services
U.S. Naval Institute
291 Wood Road
Annapolis, MD 21402-5034
Telephone: (800) 233-8764
Fax: (410) 571-1703
Web address: www.usni.org